SUCCESS
THROUGH BETTER
MEMORY

SUCCESS
THROUGH BETTER
MEMORY

A Two-Week Program for Boosting Your Memory Power

Eric M. Bienstock, Ph.D.

A Perigee Book

Perigee Books
are published by
The Putnam Publishing Group
200 Madison Avenue
New York, NY 10016

Facial drawings by Howard Roberts.

Library of Congress Cataloging-in-Publication Data

Bienstock, Eric M.
    Success through better memory: a two-week program for boosting
your memory power/by Eric M. Bienstock.

        p. cm.—(The Practical handbook series)
    Bibliography: p.
    1. Mnemonics. 2. Success. I. Title. II. Series.
    ISBN 0-399-51577-1
    BF385.B59   1989   89-8420 CIP
    153.1′4—dc20

Printed in the United States of America

1 2 3 4 5 6 7 8 9 10

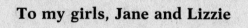

To my girls, Jane and Lizzie

Contents

BEFORE YOU BEGIN

WHAT THIS PROGRAM CAN DO FOR YOU

Memory is important. Thousands of human activities depend on memory. Without a memory we would not be able to do all the routine daily tasks needed just to survive. Some, such as tying our shoes or taking a shower or picking up the telephone, depend mostly on muscle memory. That is, our muscles have remembered what to do so that we don't have to think consciously about what to do. And that's a good thing, for imagine what life would be like if we had to think deliberately about each of the thousands of routine tasks we perform each day!

But there is another sort of memory, which makes more use of our rational brain—our reasoning power—perhaps even a different part of our brain entirely. The memory required to memorize a new telephone number, or to remember the name and occupation of a person you've just met or where you last parked your car is the sort of memory we'll be working on in this program.

Notice the word "program." Improving your memory is not a matter of just reading a book and learning what memory is all about. Certainly it's important to understand how memory works, but to actually improve your memory you must learn and practice memory *techniques*.

You have in your hands a *program* for memory improvement, not just an interesting book about memory. Throughout this program you will read, think, and learn, and then apply what you learn by doing practical exercises; by doing so you commit yourself to building your actual, usable memory power.

And that power can be considerable. Imagine, for example, being able to memorize your entire file of names, addresses, and phone numbers, or deliver a half-hour presentation without notes, or remember the names and occupations of a roomful of strangers, or memorize a list of twenty appointments without the aid of a calendar!

Certainly you know that all of these feats are possible, and much, much more. You've seen those "memory tricks" performed on television: a performer goes into the audience and correctly recites the names of 500 or so people, having met them only briefly before air time.

Well, it isn't magic. It's a matter of learning and becoming extremely skilled at tried and proven memory techniques.

You may not be interested in impressing others with a superior memory (by memorizing your city's entire telephone book, for example), but it's nice to know there's almost no limit to how much the human brain can actually remember. It gives hope to those who'd just like to be able to get along without having to carry around dozens of scraps of written reminders, or no longer to be embarrassed by forgetting an important appointment, or not being able to remember where we put our eyeglasses!

You also need a good memory if you want to be more successful. If you're a student you already know how important it is to be able to remember what you read in your texts or hear in your classes. If you're a salesperson you know how remembering bits of personal information about a new client can win new business. If you're a busy executive you know how important it is to remember your appointments, or quote significant numbers about your company's operations. If you're an active homemaker you know how vital it is to keep on schedule and not forget all those errands you've got to do. If you're a secretary you can imagine how efficient you could be by memorizing phone numbers, schedules, names, faces and jobs. In fact, your success in any area of life could be enhanced through a better memory.

One other point: A side benefit of doing this program is that it will actually help sharpen your thinking skills, and in particular, your creativity. I know this to be true because of something I've discovered from many years of seminar work and consulting for corporations and schools on creative thinking skills. The secret ingredient is *use:* The more frequently and intensely you stretch the present bounds of your mind the more you will be able to do so the next time.

So prepare yourself for some stimulation of the gray cells!

HOW TO USE THIS PROGRAM

I've designed this program so that, on the average, it can be completed over a two-week period if you invest between one and a half and two hours per day. You will spend some of your time reading, some of it reflecting, and some of it doing practice exercises.

If you cannot devote 90 to 120 minutes each day, then consider spreading the program out over, say, four weeks instead of two.

If you don't want to commit yourself to the entire program in sequence, at least read this introductory material and then do Days 1, 2, and 3, which contain many of the basic skills used later. Then you can skip to the sections that interest you most.

If you find that you need to take more than two weeks, or need more than 120 minutes per day, that's perfectly fine too. You can always go back at any point and redo certain exercises, or even an entire section. The important thing is that you actually develop the skills being worked on, before moving on to the next section or day.

It is *not* a good idea to try to complete the program in less than the prescribed two weeks, for this is a skills-building program that requires that you practice over time. If you find yourself "zipping through" the program, use your extra time to do some extra practice. Without going ahead to the next day's lesson, you can just do more exercises, or harder exercises, to practice building speed and power in the techniques you've already learned. It's a good idea to do the exercises in a spiral notebook you use only for this program. That way you can check back and monitor your progress.

Nine of the 14 days are devoted to learning new techniques and applying those techniques to common memory problems. Another three days are devoted exclusively to review and practice of the techniques you've learned on the previous few days.

Each of the learning days is broken down into segments separated by "break points." Each break point is clearly marked on the page. At this point you should take a short break. Observe the break point just as well as you follow any other instruction in the program.

Each of the learning segments should require 20 to 30 minutes of your *concentrated* attention. Then, when you come to the break point, take a 10- to 15-minute break to do something else (or nothing). It is important that you follow this routine, for experience has shown this to be an effective learning strategy. If you try to do more and rest less, it will only "burn out your circuits." It's always better to use shorter bursts of learning and longer rests that the other way around. Be good to yourself. You're learning something new, and learning should be fun!

Pay special attention to the first and last days of the program. The first day covers some basic principles you'll be using throughout the program, and the last day is devoted to an overall summary and a final self-test of your memory abilities.

And that brings us to your first activity: a self-test to determine your present memory capabilities. This will give you an idea of how effective your memory power is right now, before beginning the program. This will also serve as a bench mark against which you'll be able to compare your performance on the final self-test at the end of the program.

"HOW GOOD IS YOUR MEMORY?" SELF-TEST

Instructions

This is a test to determine your present memory capabilities. To get an accurate result, be sure you are sitting in a comfortable place and you will not be interrupted for about an hour. Go through the test only once. These questions will be used again in the final self-test, so don't study any of this material once you've finished the test.

Don't get upset if you have difficulty—this test is for your eyes only! Scoring will be explained at the end. Try to enjoy it.

1. Study the following list of 20 items for two minutes. Then cover the list and write down the items in your notebook in any order.

1. Window	11. Fireman
2. Skunk	12. Lobster
3. Frankfurter	13. Ecstasy
4. Wheel	14. Worker
5. Door knob	15. Perfume
6. Water	16. Button
7. Diamond	17. Adult
8. Barnyard	18. Photograph
9. Eye	19. Winter
10. Skirt	20. Tailor

2. Study the following list of 20 chores for three minutes. Then cover the list and write down the chores in your notebook *in proper order*.

1. Pay the phone bill	11. Change the light bulb
2. Call the plumber	12. Eat lunch
3. Type a letter	13. Plan your weekend
4. Read the annual report	14. Look for the missing report
5. Fix the blinds	15. Order new stationery
6. Send a fax	16. Call the messenger service
7. Call your broker	17. Think about vacation
8. Send a telegram	18. Study your speech
9. Call the bank	19. Call home
10. Turn off the computer	20. Write tomorrow's to-do list

3. Read through the following passage once only, at your normal reading rate. Then, without looking back at it, write down in your notebook 12 main ideas from the passage. (This material has been excerpted from the Charter of the United Nations.)

There shall be a Secretariat comprising a secretary general and such staff as the organization may require. The secretary general shall be appointed by the General Assembly on the recommendation of the Security Council. He shall be the chief administrative officer of the organization.

The secretary general shall act in that capacity in all meetings of the General Assembly, of the Security Council, of the Economic and Social Council and of the Trusteeship Council, and shall perform such other functions as are entrusted to him by these organs. The secretary general shall make an annual report to the General Assembly on the work of the organization.

The secretary general may bring to the attention of the Security Council any matter which in his opinion may threaten the maintenance of international peace and security.

In the performance of their duties the secretary general and the staff shall not seek or receive instructions from any Government or from any other authority external to the organization. They shall refrain from any action which might reflect on their position as international officials responsible only to the organization.

Each member of the United Nations undertakes to respect the

exclusively international character of the responsibilities of the secretary general and the staff, and not to seek to influence them in the discharge of their responsibilities.

The staff shall be appointed by the secretary general under regulations established by the General Assembly.

Appropriate staffs shall be permanently assigned to the Economic and Social Council, the Trusteeship Council, and, as required, to other organs of the United Nations. These staffs shall form a part of the Secretariat.

The paramount consideration in the employment of the staff and in the determination of the conditions of service shall be the necessity of securing the highest standards of efficiency, competence and integrity. Due regard shall be paid to the importance of recruiting the staff on as wide a geographical basis as possible.

4. For two minutes, study the following eight faces and their matching names and occupations. Then turn the page and fill in the correct name and occupation under each face.

name: Mr. Garfield
occupation: Salesman

name: Ms. O'Hara
occupation: Librarian

name: Ms. Charles
occupation: Social worker

name: Mr. Stevens
occupation: President

name: Mr. Suarez
occupation: Letter carrier

name: Ms. Powers
occupation: Consultant

name: Mrs. Calabrese
occupation: Office manager

name: Mr. Hoffman
occupation: Computer technician

name:

occupation:

name:

occupation:

name:

occupation:

name:

occupation:

name:

occupation:

name:

occupation:

name:
occupation:

name:
occupation:

5. Below are five 15-digit numbers. Taking each one in turn spend one minute committing it to memory; then cover up the number and write it down correctly in your notebook.

Number List

1. 284730673496871
2. 984520581658204
3. 832534958309223
4. 236583619582406
5. 878765450188434

6. Spend three minutes studying the following list of items and prices. Then cover up the list and recall the correct price of each item.

Item	Price ($)
Coaxial cable	39.95
Box of disks	14.95
Ream of paper	24.50
Black ribbon	9.95
Cleaning fluid	11.25
Laser cartridge	110.00
Keyboard	99.95
Thesaurus	4.50

7. Take five minutes to memorize the following list of people and their telephone numbers. Then cover up the list and in your notebook fill in the correct number for each person listed.

Telephone List

The bank	465-8876
TV repairman	678-0936
Police station	861-0090
Your boss	284-9461
Your best friend	897-5612
The garage	371-4729
Your doctor	775-3618
The hospital	889-1633
The printer	216-9642
Your accountant	664-1300

Recall List

The printer
Your best friend
The bank
The garage
Your accountant
The hospital
Your boss
TV repairman
Police station
Your doctor

8. Study the following list of dates and events for two minutes. Then cover up the list and answer the questions that follow.

Events List

November 19, 1863: The Gettysburg Address was delivered.
June 25, 1950: North Korea invaded South Korea.
April 30, 1789: George Washington inaugurated President.
May 6, 1937: The dirigible *Hindenburg* exploded.
March 15, 1767: President Andrew Jackson was born.

Answer these questions about the preceding "Events List."

When was George Washington inaugurated President?
When was the Gettysburg Address delivered?
When was President Andrew Jackson born?
When was the *Hindenburg* destroyed?
When did North Korea invade South Korea?

9. Study the following list of appointments for two minutes. Then recall the entire schedule.

Thursday 10:00 A.M.: Meet with accountant
Monday 3:00 P.M.: Staff meeting
Wednesday 1:30 P.M.: Lunch with new client
Tuesday 9:15 A.M.: Doctor's appointment
Friday 7:00 P.M.: Partners' dinner
Tuesday 10:45 A.M.: Buy new suit

Scoring the test: Use the following guidelines, then record your score.

Question #1: One point for each item recalled. Maximum 20 points.
Question #2: One point for each item recalled. One additional point for each item recalled in its correct position. Maximum 40 points.
Question #3: Two points for each main idea recalled. You must use your own judgment in scoring. If you have difficulty, ask someone else to score it for you. Maximum 24 points.
Question #4: Three points for each name correctly matched. Three points for each occupation correctly matched. Maximum 48 points.
Question #5: Two points for each number correctly recalled (all digits must be correct and in proper order). Maximum 10 points.
Question #6: Two points for each correct price. Maximum 16 points.
Question #7: Two points for each correct number. Maximum 20 points.
Question #8: Two points for each correct date. Maximum 10 points.
Question #9: Two points for each correct appointment. Maximum 12 points.

Question #	Maximum Possible	Your Score
1.	20	_____
2.	40	_____
3.	24	_____
4.	48	_____
5.	10	_____
6.	16	_____
7.	20	_____
8.	10	_____
9.	12	_____
Totals	200	_____

Note: You can convert your score to a percentage by dividing it by 2. For example, a score of 120 represents 60 percent and a score of 121 represents 60.5 percent. The importance of the score, however, is as a baseline for comparing your second score (when you've finished this program).

Warning! Do not use this test material for practice. You will use it again as the final self-test at the end of the program.

DAY 1

HOW YOUR MEMORY WORKS

There are three general areas of memory we need to examine. To borrow phrases from the computer industry, let's call these areas "input," "storage," and "output."

Input refers to the way we first take in the information we wish to remember; psychologists call this "encoding." Storage refers to the way the information is actually maintained in the brain, and output refers to the way we try to recall the stored information.

The most important of these three stages, for our purposes, is the first; input (encoding). The second most important is output and the least important is storage.

Storage of information in the brain does not concern us much since there is little we can do to influence the process. This is true despite all of the recent brain research on left-brain and right-brain differences, specialization of brain cells, etc. The way the brain stores information is still a great mystery. Once we've input the information, there is nothing we can do to force our brain to store it in any particular way. It would be nice, for example, if we could instruct our brain to put a certain list "on top of the pile" so that we could find it quickly later, or a particular name in a particular file folder in a particular drawer, for easy access a year from now. But we can't because we really don't yet understand how the brain stores what it knows.

As for the output stage, this is of some interest, for the more we can make use of certain output strategies the better our chance of successful recall will be. We can learn to remember something over the long term, for example, by regularly practicing recalling it. (You will get a better idea of how output strategies can be used when doing the practice exercises.)

We are most concerned with the input stage, for we can have the most influence over this activity. It has been demonstrated many times through carefully designed laboratory experiments that the better we encode the information the better we will be able to remember it, whether in the long or short term. The reasons for this are not completely known. But most of the theories suggest that the particular way we initially input the information has a direct effect on the way the information is actually stored in the brain. The more efficiently the information is initially stored the easier it will be to recall it later.

To many people this would seem fairly obvious. After all, it works the same way with a manual filing system: If you file something alphabetically, later you will be able to find it more easily than if you had filed it out of sequence.

Obvious or not, the fact is that most of us do not normally pay much attention to the way we initially input information into our brains. The whole point of this program then, is to learn to use specific, proven techniques when we initially input new information into our brains, in order to be able to recall that information with ease and speed later.

SHORT-TERM AND LONG-TERM MEMORY

We will not focus in any special way on memory for the very long term, such as remembering what happened on a particular day a year later. We will be concerned mostly with memory in the relatively short term—more accurately, the near term—such as memorizing a list of things you must do tomorrow, or a telephone number the operator has just read to you.

But your input strategy should be pretty much the same, whether you are intending to remember something for the long term or the short term. The memory techniques you'll learn in this program are so effective that you'll feel comfortable using them even for something you consider so vital that you must remember it for the rest of your life! It would be rare that you would try to remember something in a different way for the long term than for the short term.

The ability to remember something for more than just the immediate moment depends mostly on how often you practice recalling the information. That is, if you need to remember something for the long term, such as a close friend's telephone number, then be sure to practice recalling it often. This frequent practice at recall will automatically keep your memory of the information strong.

There are occasions, however, when it's better to make a written reminder for yourself than to try to make use of your memory, especially long-term memory. Sometimes it just isn't necessary to memorize the information. For example, suppose you receive an invitation to a friend's wedding to take place in three months. There's little to be gained from memorizing all of the details, such as the address and driving directions. On the day of the wedding, however, you might indeed want to memorize the address and driving directions so that you don't have to try reading them while driving!

The point is that even though you could use your memory power, particularly after boosting it with this program, there are times when it just isn't a good use of your time and energy to rely solely on memory. Or it may be premature to commit something to memory. Sometimes you might just be better off writing yourself a note.

On the other hand, one of the objectives of this program is to learn to live without having to *depend* on writing things down, particularly since there are so many times when it's not even possible to stop to write yourself a note. Suppose, for example, you're standing on a crowded bus on your way to work one morning and suddenly remember an important phone call you've got to make at lunch time. It wouldn't be possible to take out a pencil and paper to write yourself a reminder, but you *could* use one of the memory techniques to be sure you won't forget to make that call.

BUILDING YOUR NATURAL MEMORY POWER, AT ANY AGE

Many theories attempt to explain why we seem to lose some of our memory power as we age. These theories fall into two general categories: those that claim that as a person ages the brain actually becomes physically less capable as a memory storage device, and those that claim it's just a matter of decreasing aptitude owing to fewer opportunities to practice the skills related to memory usage.

If you are a firm believer in the first explanation you'll always feel you're fighting a losing battle against the effects of time, and no amount of memory skill practice will change that attitude. You might as well stop reading; go out and stock up on note pads, pencils, and a good hand-held tape recorder and tapes.

But if you want to *do* something about your memory abilities, you can indeed increase your current capacity to remember!

This has been demonstrated time and time again. In fact, some brain researchers believe that failure to remember something, regardless of the age of the subject, does not indicate a failure of the brain's storage capability but rather a failure in the output process; that is, a "recall failure." The implication is that we haven't really forgotten, we've just not been successful at recalling. And, as mentioned earlier, the ability to recall stored information is directly related to how well that information was initially input, which in turn is a function of the memory skills used.

So the choice is yours. Either you believe that nothing can be done to stop a deteriorating brain and that it is only inevitable that your memory abilities will continue to weaken, or else you believe that by learning and practicing certain techniques you can actually develop your memory in much the same way as you can develop one of your body's muscles.

And this brings us to the question of attitude. Clearly it's important to have a positive attitude before continuing with this program. You want to be optimistic, and, as in many other activities, if you believe you can succeed then you probably will.

But there is another aspect of attitude that is of importance here. As we'll see later, many of the memory techniques will depend on your ability to be open-minded, to fantasize, to let your mind go wild, to be actively creative in your thinking. The techniques will not work for you if you're skeptical, narrow-minded, mentally lazy, or unwilling to try to be imaginative.

Notice the words "try to be imaginative." Certainly not everyone has the same degree of imagination. That's okay, for you'll find that your imaginative capacity will increase as a result of doing this program. But you've got to start off with a *willingness* to work at it.

Personal motivation is also important. Do you remember the last time you were really eager to do something? Perhaps it was something simple like seeing a particular movie starring your favorite actor. Maybe you even ran out in the rain and stood on line for an hour—just to fulfill your burning desire! Or perhaps you worked overtime for three weeks straight so you could afford to buy that new coat you just had to have! Well, those are examples of what personal motivation can do. When motivation is great enough, obstacles don't exist.

So before continuing, spend a few moments thinking about why you want to increase your memory power. What will you use it for? What are your practical, daily needs that depend on memory? What specific benefits will you enjoy once you've improved your memory? How good do you really want to get?

If you really desire a good memory, then chances are you will soon have one!

MEMORY IS A LEARNABLE SKILL, REGARDLESS OF INTELLIGENCE OR EDUCATION

If you accept the notion that developing a powerful memory is much like developing any other skill, then we should be able to identify certain common characteristics of "skills." Suppose, for example, we compare building memory skills to building tennis skills.

In learning tennis it's important to be able to apply *deliberate focus of attention* to what you are doing at the moment. You can't have your mind on something else. You must focus all of your attention, in a deliberate way (i.e., not accidentally), on how you hit the ball, where you place your feet, etc. If you've taken lessons your instructor may even have told you that you must see the ball actually touch the racquet. This is a technique for forcing you deliberately to focus your attention on the very point of impact.

It works pretty much the same way in learning memory skills. You must focus your attention, deliberately, on what it is you want to remember later. When you first look at the information you have to memorize, you must apply your memory principles and techniques in a very deliberate way. This means being aware of what principles and techniques you are using, and how. For example, when trying to learn a new name and face (as you'll learn later), you must focus your attention on that face in a very deliberate way. This is probably quite different from the casual way most of us look at each other when being introduced.

Of course, once you've become a real memory expert many of these behaviors will come about more easily. Just as the tennis expert seems to do certain things without much effort, once you've built your memory skills you'll be able to do certain things without having to work quite so hard. The skills will become part of your regular, normal behavior.

Another aspect of skill learning is *regular practice.* You cannot expect to become a good tennis player without regular, serious practice. Practice helps to build skills because it teaches new patterns to our muscles, nerves, and brains. Once we've learned these new patterns we can respond more quickly and we can broaden our base, thus allowing us to learn more and more. In tennis, for example, by regularly practicing the backhand stroke against a wall we develop the ability to respond more effectively to a shot to our backhand side; once mastered, the backhand stroke allows us to learn the backhand smash and the backhand lob.

In learning memory techniques, regular practice trains those parts of our brain responsible for memory functions. It trains us to respond more quickly, and therefore more efficiently. It also increases our capacity to remember, allowing very skilled memory artists to remember what may seem like a limitless amount of information.

When we are young we get regular memory-skill practice from being in school. As we age, however, there is usually less demand on us to regularly practice using our memory. (And of course as adults we can more easily afford things like calculators, tape recorders, and even secretaries to remember things for us!) So if we want to sharpen—or even just maintain—our memory skills, we need to do some regular practice.

But practice creates boredom if there is no *practical application*. In tennis, practical application would be simply having a game. It is the idea of having a game that gives all of that regular practice some meaning. Without the promise of a game sometime in the future, few people would continue to practice their tennis strokes against a wall.

Similarly, it is pointless to be an expert at memory techniques if you have no need to apply them. You must apply what you learn in this program to your everyday life. Don't just do the exercises and then forget about the techniques. Look for situations in your life where you can apply the techniques on a daily basis. That will motivate you and keep your skills sharp.

Detachment from ego is also important when learning skills. This means, in tennis for example, that you understand that you are simply building skills, and that it is no reflection on your intelligence, virility, personality, soul, or worthiness as a human being when you make mistakes; your definition as a human being does not depend on how well or poorly you can learn the skills of tennis.

In much the same way it's important to view learning memory skills as an intellectual exercise, with little consequence to the universe other than some small improvement in your personal happiness. If you adopt this attitude, then you will more easily be able to evaluate your progress realistically and not get down on yourself if you're not perfect in everything you try. If you don't do well on some of the exercises, try to figure out why. If you need more time or more practice, give it to yourself. With this attitude you are most certainly going to get something valuable from this program—enough to make some difference in the overall quality of your life!

BASIC MEMORY PRINCIPLES OF ASSOCIATION, IMAGINATION, ORGANIZATION

Before tackling the specific memory techniques, it's important to understand certain principles underlying those techniques. This will help you to understand *why* the techniques work in addition to *how* they work.

The Basic Memory Principles are: association, imagination, and organization.

Association refers to how we connect new information with something we already know. Association is important in all learning activities, not just building memory skill, for it is based on the way the human brain operates.

The human brain is essentially a pattern-making and pattern-using system. That is, it tries to create connections, or patterns, between and among the billions and billions of bits of information it must store. Then, when new information is introduced, the brain tries to connect that new information with what it already knows, forming a new or slightly modified pattern. In other words, the human brain looks at new information in terms of how it can connect that new information to already existing patterns.

The implication for developing memory skills is this:

If we want to memorize something, we need to associate it with something that is already firmly implanted in our memory. Furthermore, if we want to memorize information that is new, unfamiliar, or obscure—such as a strange name or an abstract concept or a collection of numbers—then we need to associate that information with something that is already known, familiar, or concrete in our minds.

Here is an example. When children are taught to read using the phonics approach, they are taught the sound of "at." Then they are taught that by placing the letter "b" in front they get the word "bat." And then if the letter "c" is used instead, they will have the word "cat," and so on. Thus, by *associating* the new words "bat" and "cat" with the already known sound of "at," the children are more easily able to learn the new words than if they had to memorize them individually and independently.

Imagination is necessary to make the mental associations strong ones. It is imagination that transforms the ordinary into the extraordinary, and it is always easier to remember things which are extraordinary. It is also imagination that enables the human brain quickly and easily to create associations between unrelated things.

As a simple example, consider the case of Jack the Ripper, the late-nineteenth-century English murderer of street prostitutes. Few people would even remember that a murderer named Jack ever existed, if it weren't for the extraordinary appellation given to him by Scotland Yard of "the Ripper." It stirs the imagination. And it easily triggers the connection in the mind between "ripper" and "killer."

Imagination can be enhanced by using any of the following:

Absurdities: A dancing tree, while an absurd image, is far more easily remembered than a run-of-the mill standing tree.

Exaggeration of size: A tree that reaches up into the clouds is more easily remembered than a normal-sized tree. Similarly, a miniature tree that can fit inside a thimble is a memorable image.

Exaggeration of quantity: It would be easier to remember millions of trees filling the landscape than a just a few.

Out of context: Trees growing out of your living room floor conjures up a more memorable image than trees growing out of the ground, their natural habitat.

Color: Multicolored trees are more easily remembered than plain green and brown trees. Just ask anyone who has gone away for a weekend in October to view the fall foliage!

Emotion: An angry tree is more vivid than an unemotional tree.

Sex: The image of two trees having sexual intercourse is an image not easily forgotten.

Action: The image of trees on the march is more memorable than trees standing still.

Sound: Trees singing "The Star-Spangled Banner" is more easily remembered than silent trees.

Taste: You will more easily remember trees that taste like chocolate than trees you can't eat.

Smell: Trees that smell like strawberries are more easily remembered than trees that have no smell.

Touch: Trees that feel like real leather when you touch them will remain in your memory more than trees you haven't touched (in your mind, of course!).

Sight: Seeing trees vividly in your mind, with all of their detail, helps to implant the image more firmly than just speculating what a tree might look like.

And now to look at the importance of *organization* in developing memory skills. Many of the memory techniques will call upon your sense of organization in many ways. For example, you will have to design several sets of personal "key words" for some of the techniques, or work with numerical schemes. This is not all that complicated, but you will not be able to do it effectively if you don't pay attention to organization. In this context organization refers to your ability to approach things in a systematic, orderly fashion.

Being organized in your daily routines can also be of valuable help in other ways. For example, if you frequently misplace things, such as your keys, you might try being more systematic about how you handle them. Suppose you select a place in your home where you *always* place your keys. Then, if you follow your own rule, you should always be able to find them. Of course you will want to pick a place that is very convenient, such as on a hook behind the front door, or in a cup on a table in the entrance foyer.

I use this kind of strategy whenever I travel on business. Upon arriving at my hotel room I quickly organize my possessions so that they will be easily available to me without my feeling like I'm living out of a suitcase, I won't have to search every crevice of the room when packing to leave, and I feel in control.

Again, I use the principles of organization by habitually putting my room key in an empty ashtray on whatever table is closest to the door, my alarm clock on the bedside table, my seminar materials on a table or chair closest to the window, my empty suitcase in the closet either above or below my hanging clothes, my toiletries bag on the sink in the bathroom, etc.

Another way to make use of organization is to pay attention to the way you put things together. The need for this will become clearer as you develop the memory techniques. But for now, consider the following list of different ways things can be organized. Things can be

- substituted for each other (exchanged).
- stuck together, permanently or temporarily.
- separated from each other, permanently or temporarily.
- merged (made the same).
- put on top of (or underneath one another).
- put inside (or outside) each other.

One final comment. There is no contradiction between organization and imagination, as some people might think. When I come into a corporate setting to teach creativity, for example, there is often some skeptical executive who thinks he will have to roll up his sleeves and "let it all loose." Not so. Imagination does not mean chaos, it just means using the brain differently.

Nor does organization mean rigidity. Organization means having a definite purpose so that we are always in control and therefore results-oriented. Organization enables us to be creative by design.

We can be very imaginative in an organized way, and we can be very organized and still have a "wild" imagination. Without organization, imagination can't be put to good use; without imagination, organization is boring! Both a vivid imagination and a strong sense of organization are vital to being able to form strong mental associations. And, as you shall soon see, this is what's required for developing memory power.

DAY 2

TECHNIQUE: THE LINK SYSTEM

The first technique to learn is called linking or the Link System. This technique has many applications and is also basic for learning many of the other techniques.

One application of linking is in memorizing a list of things in a particular order. For example, you could use this technique to memorize a shopping list. Later we will also use this technique to remember a "to-do" list.

Linking is very simple. You create a "mental link" between two items, which are usually unrelated, by creating some *meaningful and memorable association* between them. You create this mental link by using the Basic Memory Principles discussed earlier. Then, to remember a list, you just have to conjure up the mental link between each pair in the list.

Before we see how this actually works with a list, let's take some time to develop the skill of creating mental links between pairs of unrelated items.

Suppose, for example, you wanted to create a mental link between "table" and "apple." At first blush you see no connection between the two items. But now try to formulate some outrageous or ridiculous fantasy that involves the two items. If it helps, close your eyes and let your imagination go wild. Form a mental scene in your mind that has color, action, taste, smell, and feel. Involve as many of your senses as possible. Pause now for a moment and try to do this.

It's best to form your own mental associations rather than use someone else's (such as mine). You will always remember your own better. So give your mind a chance to come up with something first. And don't worry, your mind really will come up with something if you give it a chance!

Back to the example. Suppose your mental link between "table" and "apple" is this: You visualize the coffee **table** in your living room with an enormous, succulent red **apple** sitting on it, taking up the entire space, being munched on by your dinner guests. You can even hear the slurping as they bite into this giant juicy fruit. (What a nice fantasy. You don't have to serve your guests dessert; they just adjourn to the living room, where they can lean over for a bite of this wonderful apple whenever they like!)

That's how linking works. Notice the use of imagination in forming the association between the two unrelated items.

A tip: When deliberately trying to tap your imagination (such as when creating mental links) it's best to stick with the first thing that comes to mind. Don't try to improve the fantasy with lots of logic. In fact, the more ridiculous the better!

That's basically how to link two items. It's simple! Now for some practice.

EXERCISE 1: Create a mental link for each of the following pairs. Don't spend more than 30 seconds on each pair—you'll actually be more effective that way.

- Milk & light bulb
- Book & shoe polish
- Steak & newspaper
- Candle & necktie
- Toast & bus
- Pillow & mustache
- Chair & love
- Happiness & politics

Hint: Notice that the last two pairs include items that are not tangible, but are abstract concepts: love, happiness, and politics. The trick to creating a mental link for an abstract concept is to associate love with a big red heart, happiness with an enormous grin, and politics with a sleazy, cigar-smoking politician. In other words, when dealing with abstract concepts you must first form an additional mental link between the abstract word and some concrete image. You consciously remember this concrete image; its abstract association sits in the background of your mind and comes to the fore only when you try to recall the item.

EXERCISE 2: Create a mental link for each of the following pairs, which involve abstract concepts. Again, spend no more than 30 seconds per pair.

- Rich & staircase
- Sick & fast
- Freedom & hot
- Hate & tall

APPLICATION: REMEMBERING A LIST OF THINGS IN ORDER

Now we're ready to link more than two items. It isn't any more difficult than what you've already done. Just create a link between each pair of items in the list by linking each new item in the list to the one you've already learned. That is, you learn the new item by linking it to an item you already know (the previous item in the list).

Here's an example. Suppose you wanted to memorize the following list of items:

Milk
Light bulb
Book
Shoe polish
Steak
Newspaper

You have, no doubt, noticed that these are the first six items from Exercise 1. Suppose these items represent your shopping list. Here, then, is how you can remember them by linking.

Milk is first (this one you just have to remember!). Next you form some silly, *illogical* link between milk (which you now know) and **light bulb,** which is a new item. For example, imagine an enormous swimming pool full of **milk** with thousands of **light bulbs** in it, bobbing up and down. Note that you *do not* want to form too *logical* a connection between milk and light bulb, such as "they are both white." While this may be true, it is too easily forgotten, for lots of things are white. The idea here is to form a ridiculous link, so that it stands out from the ordinary.

Pause here for a moment and think about that last comment. Ask yourself this question: Which is more vivid in your mind, the image of thousands of light bulbs bobbing around in an enormous swimming pool of milk, or two things that are white? You must truly believe that the more absurd is more easily remembered, before continuing with this program!

Now ponder this statement for a moment: It is always easier to remember things that are out of the ordinary, absurd, or unexpected than it is to remember things that are ordinary, logical, or expected.

Continuing with the example, now that you've linked milk to light bulb, you can remember light bulb if you can remember milk. That is, just by remembering milk your mind will *automatically* remember light bulb because it cannot forget the ridiculous image of thousands of light bulbs in a swimming pool full of milk.

The next step is to create a link between **light bulb** and **book.** Again, do *not* be tempted by logic to say something sensible like "You can read a book under a light bulb." Instead, imagine something as ridiculous as this: Inside a **light bulb** there is a tiny person reading a tiny **book.** Now you have a link between these two items, so that if you can recall **light bulb** then you will also recall **book** because your mind cannot forget the absurd image of a tiny **book** inside a **light bulb.**

Next we need to form a mental link between **book** and **shoe polish.** Perhaps you might imagine a **book** whose cover is dripping brown **shoe polish.**

For the next link, between **shoe polish** and **steak,** you might visualize using **shoe polish** to baste a **steak.** And for the final link you might imagine your waiter serving you a big juicy **steak** on a **newspaper** instead of on a plate.

If you've got those individual fantasies *vividly implanted* in your mind, then you can easily remember all six items by just remembering the first one, **milk.** The others will come to you automatically (particularly when *you* are the one who creates the fantasies). For the word **milk** conjures up in your mind the silly image of floating **light bulbs.** Then, **light bulb** makes you think of a tiny **book** inside it; **book** triggers the fantasy of dripping **shoe polish,** which in turn makes you think of basting **steaks.** And finally, **steak** triggers the gruesome image of a waiter serving you one on **newspaper.**

Linking works because you use the Basic Memory Principles to create the absurd associations. Your mind more easily remembers these absurd associations than it does the mundane words such as "milk," "light bulb," "book," etc. Also, the very act of creating your own silly fantasies forces you to focus deliberately on each of the items, even if only for a moment. This act of *deliberate focus* helps to implant the item in your mind.

Sometimes you might find yourself creating a *single* fantasy to link your entire list of items. For example, here is a fantasy you could have used for the previous example:

A cow is giving **milk** into a huge **light bulb** (instead of a pail). The **light bulb** is being balanced on an enormously thick **book,** which is floating in a vat of **shoe polish.** The person doing the milking (the farmer?) is also painting **steaks** with the **shoe polish,** the purpose of which is to remind the cow of what might happen if she refuses to cooperate. Then the **steaks** are wrapped in **newspaper** and taken to market.

Notice how this links all of the items in a fantasy that contains a common thread, so that in the end all six items are part of the same fanciful scene. It doesn't have to be that way, and in fact when you did Exercise 1 you were probably not trying to link one pair of items to the next. But when you start out knowing that you've got to link several items, you might find yourself developing a single fantasy by weaving each succeeding item into the story. Don't force it, but if it happens let it happen. The important thing is to link each item to the previous one by making it fanciful, absurd, and exaggerated.

You may at this point be thinking that linking seems to require a lot of words. But it doesn't really. It certainly takes a good deal of explanation to describe on paper how it works, but when you do it your mind creates the images very quickly, especially when you are skilled at it. You will find it far easier to do than to explain.

So now for some skill-building exercises. You may find it helpful, at first, to talk out loud or draw pictures as you think. That's fine for now, while you're learning. Eventually, however, you want to become skilled at relying on nothing but your mind's images.

You'll notice in these exercises that you are asked to do more in less time for each succeeding exercise. This is done deliberately. As in developing any other skill, you will eventually be able to use the Link System to memorize large numbers of items in a surprisingly short period of time, and with relatively little effort. The key, of course is *practice*—so be sure to do all of the exercises as instructed!

EXERCISE 3: Use the Link System to memorize the following list of items. Time yourself—take no more than five minutes. Then try recalling the list, in order, by visualizing your links.

> Cake
> Automobile
> Magazine
> Paint
> Computer
> Banana
> Bed
> Key

BREAK POINT

EXERCISE 4: Give yourself three minutes to implant this list in your mind using linking. When you are done, cover the list and write down in your notebook all of the items in order.

Column 1   Column 2

> Elephant
> Radio
> Nose
> Asparagus
> Side walk
> Hair
> Coffee
> Typewriter
> Rose
> Lateness

EXERCISE 5: Memorize the following list of items in two minutes using the Link System. Then cover the list and write down in your notebook all of the items in order.

Column 1	Column 2
Bread	
Paper clips	
Salad	
Patience	
Spoon	
Boss	
String	
Sadness	
Meadow	
Movie	

EXERCISE 6: Memorize the following list of items *in one minute* using the Link System. Then cover the list and write down, *in one minute*, all of the items in order.

Column 1	Column 2
Flower	
Stapler	
Building	
Cup	
Joy	
Cake	
Intelligent	
Scissors	
Sky	
Plastic	
Limousine	
Fingernail	

One of the keys to remembering something is not necessarily how much *time* you spending thinking about it, but how *hard* you *focus* on it. It's more effective to focus hard on something for five seconds than to focus lazily for five minutes. With practice, therefore, you should be able to memorize long lists in relatively short periods of time.

EXERCISE 7: The purpose of this exercise is to work on building speed using the Link System. Here's how it should be done: You will open a dictionary to any page. Then run down the page and link each word you encounter. (Skip any word whose meaning you do not know, or any word that is trivial, such as "the." The idea is to quickly pick some fairly tangible words at random.) Stop when you've used up one minute. Then, without looking at the dictionary page, write down all of the words in order. Make a note of how long it takes you to recall the words.

Do this exercise three times, using a different page or section each time, and then answer the following questions for each list:

1. How many words were you able to link in one minute?
2. How many words were you able to correctly recall, in order?
3. How long did it take you to recall the list?

Take note of your progress and give yourself a hearty "Congratulations!" You've begun to master the secret of your mind's natural memory power!

BREAK POINT

APPLICATION: REMEMBERING A "TO DO" LIST

Now that you've learned to use the Link System to memorize lists of items, you're ready to apply it to another common situation: remembering a list of things to do, commonly called a "to do" list.

This method is basically the same as memorizing a list of *things*, except that now the list contains *verbs* (action words), such as "*go to* the bank" or "*pick up* the laundry."

Most of the time you can ignore the action words—remembering the word "bank," for example, would probably be good enough to remind you go to there. In some cases, however, you might need to remember the particular action, such as "pick up the laundry" as opposed to "bring in the laundry."

In such cases you simply include the action in your outrageous fantasy. So when you create your mental image for the object "laundry" you include the action "pick up" in a fanciful way. You might, for example, imagine yourself lifting a globe full of dirty laundry above your head (like the image of Atlas holding up the world!).

In each of the following exercises, practice incorporating the action words into your mental images. In actual practice, of course, you might not always need to do this. But even then it's better just to automatically include the action words than to spend time trying to decide whether you need them.

EXERCISE 8: Memorize the following to-do list in three minutes, using the Link System. Then cover the list and write down in your notebook all of the chores in proper order.

Take out the garbage
Bring clothes to the cleaner's
Post the mail
Buy the newspaper
Make a deposit at the bank
Pick up your friend at the station
Order a pizza for delivery
Call your father
Write to grandmother
Listen to music on the radio
Change the sheets
Go to bed early

EXERCISE 9: Memorize the following list of things to do *in two minutes* using the Link System. Then, with the list covered, write it down in correct order in your notebook *in one minute*.

Order a dozen roses
Refill the stapler
Call the copier repairman
Type a letter
Pay the bills
Send a telegram
Read your boss's memo
Place a want-ad in the newspaper
Order a taxi
Reorganize your desk
Write a note to the cleaning lady
Change the typewriter ribbon

EXERCISE 10: In one minute or less, memorize the following to-do list. Then, while covering the list, write it down in correct order in your notebook as fast as you can.

Call the printer
Write a memo to your secretary
Read the day's finance news
Sign the salary checks
Work on next quarter's budget
Read the new marketing plan
Choose a restaurant for lunch
Meet with your staff
Attend a lunch meeting
Call your mother
Plan tomorrow's activities
Pick up Chinese food on the way home

Linking is probably the most important skill you can get from this program. By itself it is a powerful technique that has numerous practical applications. And, as you shall see throughout this program, it is also a basic skill underlying many of the other powerful techniques.

Use the Link System from now on whenever you have a list of things to remember, whether a shopping list, a to-do list, or whatever. By deliberately using it in your daily routines you will automatically be practicing the skill, and as a result will get better at it, eventually being able to remember longer lists in shorter time and with less effort. Before long, you'll be using it so automatically you might not even realize it at times. You'll have a super memory by hardly trying!

Since memory is a learnable skill, the more you use it the better you will get. So *look* for opportunities to use your memory rather than depending on writing things down.

DAY 3

TECHNIQUE: THE NUMBER RHYME SYSTEM

The Number Rhyme Technique is one of the basic "peg systems" of memory. A peg system for memory works just like a peg system in the hallway for hanging coats. Imagine a long board with ten pegs hanging in your hallway. As people come to visit they hang their coats on the pegs. While the coats may change from day to day, the pegs always remain the same— there is the first peg (closest to the door), the second peg, and so on.

A memory peg system works in much the same way. You memorize a list of pegs, say ten of them. You learn these pegs well, so that they are as much a part of your knowledge as your address or phone number. Then, to memorize a list of ten (new) items, you *link* each of the new items to one of your memory pegs. Since you already know your ten pegs, you will automatically be reminded of the ten new items through each of your linking fantasies.

Your first task is to create your own memory pegs which rhyme with the numbers one through ten. Since it's always best if you create your own personal associations, take a few minutes now to try it out. In your notebook write the figures 1 to 10 in a column, and write down next to each number a word that rhymes with it, for example, "1—gun." Keep it as short, simple, and as tangible as possible.

Number	Number Rhyme Peg
1	
2	
etc.	

Below is a suggested list of words to choose from, just in case you had some difficulty. If one of these words appeals to you more than one you had originally written down, then by all means go back to your list and make the change.

Common Number Rhyme Pegs

    1—gun, sun, bun, nun
    2—shoe, pew, crew
    3—tree, knee, flea, sea
    4—door, floor, boar, drawer
    5—hive, dive, chive, jive
    6—sticks, bricks, ticks
    7—heaven, leaven
    8—gate, bait, date, weight
    9—vine, wine, twine, line
    10—hen, den, men, pen, wren

Now that you have your number rhyme pegs you must learn them, and learn them very well!

EXERCISE 1: Sit in a comfortable chair and close your eyes. Say out loud, "one, ____; two, ____; three, ____" and so on, saying your rhyme word for each number where the blank appears. Visualize the object as you say its name. Do this five times.

(Saying things out loud often helps to store the information better in the mind.)

EXERCISE 2: Follow the instructions for Exercise 1, but say the list in reverse order.

EXERCISE 3: Follow the instructions for Exercise 2, but pick numbers at random.

EXERCISE 4: Repeat Exercises 1, 2, and 3, but do them silently.

APPLICATION: REMEMBERING A LIST IN ANY ORDER

Now that you've learned your number rhyme pegs it's time to apply them to memorizing a list of things. Here's an example. Suppose you wanted to memorize the following list of items:

1. Milk
2. Light bulb
3. Book
4. Shoe polish
5. Steak
6. Newspaper
7. Candle
8. Necktie
9. Toast
10. Bus

You will recognize this as the same list of items we tackled when first learning the Link System. Instead of linking each item with the next item on the list, however, we form a link between each item in the list and a number rhyme peg—the peg that corresponds to the number of the item. So if your number rhyme peg for 1 is "gun" you need to form a mental link between **gun** and **milk.** Perhaps you visualize a "milk gun" that squirts milk, just as a child's water gun squirts water.

In a similar way, you need to form a mental link for each item, in order. It might go something like this (of course your number rhyme pegs may differ from these):

1. Gun	Milk	A child's **gun** that squirts **milk**
2. Shoe	Light bulb	A **shoe**-shaped **light bulb** that lights when you pull on the laces
3. Tree	Book	A **tree** with **books** for leaves
4. Door	Shoe polish	A **door** painted with **shoe polish**
5. Hive	Steak	A bee**hive** made of red juicy **steak**
6. Sticks	Newspaper	A pile of **sticks** made of tightly rolled-up **newspaper**
7. Heaven	Candle	A **heaven** full of clouds, each holding a **candle** (clouds as candle holders)
8. Gate	Necktie	A front **gate** with **neckties** for slats
9. Vine	Toast	**Vines** served on **toast** (a new delicacy!)
10. Hen	Bus	A **hen** driving a **bus** full of other hens

Now you can easily recall any of the ten items in the list, *in any order*. Suppose, for example, you want to remember the seventh item (without looking, of course). My number rhyme peg for **seven** is **"heaven,"** which conjures up my fantasy of clouds as **candle** holders. And so now I know that the seventh item in the list is candle.

Similarly, if you asked me for the second item in the list I would say to myself, "Two . . . shoe . . . a shoe-shaped light bulb with laces as pull strings. So the second item is light bulb." And I would be vividly imagining this picture in my mind as I traced the link silently to myself.

You must, of course, know your personal number rhyme pegs very well for this technique to work.

Now, you might be wondering, "Isn't it easy to confuse one association with another, from a previous list you learned?" For example, if I link **seven** to **heaven** to **candle** now, what will happen if later I try to link **seven** to **heaven** to, say, **typewriter?** That is, we might have these two cases:

Case 1: seven → heaven → candle
Case 2: seven → heaven → typewriter

Let's look carefully at what is going on. First of all, your link of **seven** to **heaven** is the same in both cases. As your number rhyme peg it never changes. You have already taken some time to memorize the connection, and as you use it more and more in actual practice, the link will strengthen even more. So the link between **seven** and **heaven** is no problem.

Now, in Case 1 you have linked **heaven** to **candle.** Let's assume that you needed to remember that link for 12 hours. The next day, not needing to remember that link any more, you make no attempt to recall **candle.** It's gone, as far as you are concerned. Of course you could probably recall it if you made the attempt, but the fact is that you do not make the attempt, for two reasons: First, you have no further need to recall it, and second, you know that trying to recall it would only strengthen that link, something you have no need or desire to do. So the link between **heaven** and **candle** has been somewhat weakened by the space of a day's time.

Later, when you create the new link in Case 2, between **heaven** and **typewriter,** you are naturally going to make it a *strong* link, because you are going to use the Basic Memory Principles and, most of all, because you are going to focus deliberately on this new link. If later you need to recall **typewriter** you will be able to do so, for its link to **heaven** (and therefore to **seven**) is much stronger than the link of **candle** to **heaven.**

This is a very important point. Pause for a moment to think about this: Since the strength of any memory association decreases with time, if you want to remember a particular association over the long term you must occasionally practice recalling it. For example, if you want to be able to remember a list of ten items for a week, you should practice recalling it perhaps three or four times each day. Conversely, if you have no further need to remember something, such as a list, do not practice recalling it.

But, you may ask, what if you actually wanted to remember **candle** for a very long time? Does that mean you can't use your number rhyme pegs for anything else? No, for several reasons. One is that after a while you will be able to drop the silly association between **heaven** and **candle.** By learning the link very well you will have learned **candle** very well, through practice recall. And once **candle** is well ingrained in your memory you will have no further need for the link. You will therefore be able to drop it and still remember **candle.**

Another reason is that, with practice, you will find yourself capable of carrying hundreds, even thousands, of silly fantasy links around in your head. You will be creating them almost instantly, and you will be dropping them almost instantly, as soon as they serve no further purpose.

The worst that can happen is that you'll forget something, but you are probably already doing that anyway!

BREAK POINT

EXERCISE 5: Give yourself three minutes to learn the following list using the Number Rhyme System. Copy the list into your notebook. Cover up the original list and write down the items in order. Then cover up the previous columns and write down the items in reverse order. Finally, write the items down in the same random order, again while covering up the previous columns.

1. Eye
2. Apple
3. Cleat
4. Shawl
5. Airplane
6. Tile
7. Umbrella
8. Fish
9. Comb
10. Wall

Now suppose you had to memorize a list of more than ten items using the Number Rhyme System. How could you do it? Well, you can't, unless you create more number rhyme pegs.

You can easily create a second set of number rhyme pegs by just attaching some silly descriptor to each of your original number rhyme pegs. For example, you might attach the word "rubber." If you were to do this to each of my ten number rhyme pegs you would get the following:

First Set of 10	Second Set of 10
1. Gun	Rubber gun
2. Shoe	Rubber shoe
3. Tree	Rubber tree
4. Door	Rubber door
5. Hive	Rubber hive
6. Sticks	Rubber sticks
7. Heaven	Rubber heaven
8. Gate	Rubber Gate
9. Vine	Rubber vine
10. Hen	Rubber Hen

So to memorize an eleventh item on a list, for example, you simply create a mental link between that item and "rubber gun."

If you needed more than 20 number rhyme pegs you could easily attach some other descriptor, such as "bright red." Of course once you use a descriptor word it becomes a special word, a reserved word that you wouldn't want to use for anything else.

Take a moment before continuing to go back to where you listed your number rhyme pegs. Head up another column with a special descriptor (such as "rubber" if you like). Say the new set of pegs out loud to see if you feel comfortable with them. Then, if you're really ambitious, you might head up another column for a third set, etc.

Now, learn your new number rhyme pegs as well as you learned your original set of ten.

EXERCISE 6: Repeat Exercise 1 for each set of new number rhyme pegs.

EXERCISE 7: Repeat Exercise 2 for each set of new number rhyme pegs.

EXERCISE 8: Repeat Exercise 3 for each set of new number rhyme pegs.

EXERCISE 9: Repeat Exercise 4 for each set of new number rhyme pegs.

EXERCISE 10: Memorize the following list of items in three minutes. Then cover up the list and recall it in order in one minute. Then, again covering up the previous columns, recall the list in reverse order, and then in random order, each time in one minute.

1. Clamp	1.	15.	13.
2. Atom	2.	14.	5.
3. Oar	3.	13.	1.
4. Plate	4.	12.	10.
5. Helicopter	5.	11.	6.
6. Frog	6.	10.	9.
7. Ruby	7.	9.	14.
8. Classroom	8.	8.	3.
9. Spring	9.	7.	12.
10. Carpet	10.	6.	7.
11. Star	11.	5.	11.
12. Tweezers	12.	4.	4.
13. Corsage	13.	3.	2.
14. Sister	14.	2.	15.
15. Rice	15.	1.	8.

EXERCISE 11: Again, learn the following list in three minutes and recall it each time in one minute. You will notice that the list contains 20 items, some of which are abstract. (If you need a refresher, look back at the Link System where we first dealt with abstractions.)

1. Rival	1.	20.		12.
2. Envelope	2.	19.		9.
3. Rope	3.	18.		20.
4. Bicycle	4.	17.		6.
5. Kangaroo	5.	16.		15.
6. Pony tail	6.	15.		17.
7. Change	7.	14.		10.
8. Spaghetti	8.	13.		5.
9. Punk	9.	12.		13.
10. Curtain	10.	11.		8.
11. Sexy	11.	10.		19.
12. Souvenir	12.	9.		4.
13. Herb	13.	8.		2.
14. Waist	14.	7.		11.
15. Check	15.	6.		7.
16. Violin	16.	5.		1.
17. Carrot	17.	4.		18.
18. Skeleton	18.	3.		14.
19. Peace	19.	2.		3.
20. Puppy	20.	1.		16.

EXERCISE 12:   The purpose of this exercise is to work on building speed with the Number Rhyme System, using the dictionary as before. Pick a page at random and run your finger down a column, picking words that you know and that are not trivial. Assign a number to each word, in order, and implant in your mind an appropriate mental link between each word and your peg. See how many words you can memorize in one minute. Then, without looking at the dictionary page, write down all of the words in some arbitrary order. Make a note of how long it takes you to recall the list. Do this exercise three times (using a different page or section each time). The first time, see how many words you can memorize in one minute. The second time, try to double that number in two minutes. The third time, try to triple that number in three minutes. Then answer the following questions.

1. How many words were you able to memorize in one minute? Two minutes? Three minutes?
2. How many words were you able to recall correctly each time?
3. How long did it take you to recall each list?

Now take your right arm, stretch it over your left shoulder, and give yourself a pat on the back. You're well on your way to having a super memory!

APPLICATION: REMEMBERING A "TO DO" LIST

You can also use the Number Rhyme System to remember a "to do" list in much the same way as we did with the Link System. The big difference, however, is that even if you forget one of the chores on the list (one of the links) you will still be able to remember the others.

As discused before, you can either incorporate the "action" word into your mental image or you can disregard it. For the purpose of the exercises, however, practice using the action words.

EXERCISE 13: Use the Number Rhyme System to memorize the following list of things to do in two minutes. Then cover up the list and write it in order in your notebook in one minute. Then, again covering up the previous columns, recall the list in random order in one minute.

1. Buy postage stamps	1.	11.
2. Buy carrots	2.	9.
3. Fix the lamp	3.	1.
4. Write a memo	4.	10.
5. Call your boss	5.	6.
6. Decide about vacation	6.	4.
7. Plan your week	7.	14.
8. Watch the news on TV	8.	2.
9. Talk to your lawyer	9.	13.
10. Iron your shirts	10.	7.
11. Call the dentist	11.	12.
12. Vacuum the carpet	12.	5.
13. Read a novel	13.	8.
14. Take a nap	14.	15.
15. Take your vitamins	15.	3.

From now on, you can use the Number Rhyme System whenever you need to remember a list of things or a list of activities. But don't stop using the Link System. Both have their advantages and disadvantages (this will be discussed on the upcoming day reserved for review and practice). But since both techniques are basic to everything else you will learn, it's important to keep up your skill level in both methods.

In general, don't be tempted to choose a particular technique as your "favorite," to be used at the exclusion of others you may learn. Instead, give yourself a chance to learn and practice *all* of the techniques in this program.

DAY 4

TECHNIQUE: THE ALPHABET SYSTEM

The Alphabet System works very much like the Number Rhyme System, that is, you create a personal set of memory pegs on which to "hang" a list of words. You can then use these pegs to remember lists of items, or "to-do" lists or even how to correctly spell certain troublesome words.

In this system, as you may have guessed, we use the alphabet instead of numbers. So your first job is to create a personal set of alphabet memory pegs.

In creating alphabet memory pegs, the trick is to pick a word that begins with the same sound as the letter. For example, for the letter "r" you could use the word "ark" and for the letter "k" you could use the word "cake," because these words start with the same sound as the letter associated with them. Sometimes you can even choose a word that is pronounced exactly as the letter, such as "jay" for the letter "j." Take a few minutes to select your alphabet memory pegs before continuing.

Letter	Alphabet Memory Peg Word
A	
B	
C	
etc.	

On the next page is a list of suggested words to choose from, just in case you had some difficulty. Or consult your dictionary for other ideas. If some other word appeals to you more, go back to your list and make the change.

Common Alphabet Word Pegs

A	Ape
B	Bee
C	Sea
D	Dean
E	Eel
F	Effort
G	Gee!
H	H-bomb
I	Eye
J	Jay (the bird)
K	Cake
L	El (elevated train)
M	M&M (the candy)
N	End (as in "rear end")
O	Oboe
P	Pea
Q	Queue (a line of people)
R	Ark
S	Eskimo
T	Tea
U	U-boat
V	Veep or VP (vice president)
W	WC (Water closet)
X	X-ray
Y	Y (YMCA—a gym)
Z	Zebra

With these pegs you can memorize a list of 26 items in order, in reverse order, or in random order. But you can easily double that capability by creating an additional 26 alphabet pegs in the same way as you did with the number rhyme pegs. You might create a second list of 26 pegs by attaching the adjective "rubber," for example, to your original pegs. In this way, you could even create a third set, or a fourth.

Before continuing, go back to your original list of 26 alphabet pegs. Create another column at the top of the page and head it with your adjective for the second set. If you are truly ambitious, you can even head up a third set of 26 as well. In any case, it's a good idea to use the same adjective you used for extending your list of number rhyme pegs. That way you only have to remember one adjective. (There are times when you can aid your memory by not giving it extra, unnecessary work to do. If you can find a trick, a way to remember less than you have to, by all means use it!)

If you used the adjective I suggested, "rubber" (and if you used my original set of 26 words), you would have the two sets of pegs, as illustrated below.

	First Set of 26		Second Set of 26
A	Ape		Rubber ape
B	Bee		Rubber bee
C	Sea		Rubber sea
D	Dean		Rubber dean
E	Eel		Rubber eel
F	Effort		Rubber effort
G	Gee!		Rubber gee!
H	H-bomb		Rubber H-bomb
I	Eye		Rubber eye
J	Jay		Rubber jay
K	Cake		Rubber cake
L	El		Rubber el
M	M&M		Rubber M&M
N	End		Rubber end
O	Oboe		Rubber oboe
P	Pea		Rubber pea
Q	Queue		Rubber queue
R	Ark		Rubber ark
S	Eskimo		Rubber Eskimo
T	Tee		Rubber tee
U	U-boat		Rubber U-boat
V	Veep or VP		Rubber veep
W	WC		Rubber WC
X	X-ray		Rubber X-ray
Y	Y		Rubber Y
Z	Zebra		Rubber zebra

Some of these require a bit of extra imagination, as they are rather abstract (e.g., rubber Y). You will need to link these with something more concrete (recall the earlier discussion about abstractions when we first looked at the Link System).

Now that you have your alphabet word pegs you must learn them. Do each of the following exercises for each list of 26 alphabet word pegs you created.

EXERCISE 1: Sit in a comfortable chair and close your eyes. Say out loud "A, ____; B, ____; C, ____" and so on, saying your alphabet word peg for each letter where the blank appears. Visualize the object as you say its name. Do this five times.

EXERCISE 2: Follow the instructions for Exercise 1, but say the list in reverse order.

EXERCISE 3: Follow the instructions for Exercise 1, but pick letters at random.

EXERCISE 4: Repeat Exercises 1, 2 and 3, but silently.

BREAK POINT

APPLICATION: REMEMBERING A LIST IN ANY ORDER

Now to apply the Alphabet System to remembering a list of items. In general, the Alphabet System can be used in the same way as the Number Rhyme System: You can recall a list of items in order, in reverse order, or in random order. The only exception is that it would be difficult to recall, say, the fifteenth item, not knowing what the fifteenth letter of the alphabet is. Of course you could learn that, but it would make the Alphabet System much more complex than it has to be.

EXERCISE 5:   Use your alphabet pegs to memorize the following list of items. Do it in five minutes or less. When you are finished, cover the list and write down in your notebook all of the items in order. Then, covering the previous lists, write down all the items in reverse order. Again, covering the previous lists, write down all of the items in any random order.

Note: In the first few exercises using the Alphabet System you will probably find it helpful to write down the appropriate letter of the alphabet as you go along. That's fine in the beginning—but then aim to do the exercises without writing at all! (To recall the list in random order, however, you probably will always need to write down the letters as you go along, to be sure you've recalled them all.)

Items	Items in Order	Reverse Order	Random Order
Benefit			
Bureaucrat			
Warrior			
Stream			
Feather			
Sheriff			
Money			
Ramp			
Sun			
Pen			
Halo			
Award			
Bull			
Apartment			
Flute			
Rhinoceros			
Ellipse			
Miracle			
Barge			
Soup			
Protection			
Rifle			
Sour			
Front			
Lawyer			
Tennis ball			

EXERCISE 6:   The purpose of this exercise is to work on building speed with the Alphabet System, using the dictionary as before. Turn to a page at random and pick a word, also at random, from that page, skipping any words whose meaning you do not know and words that are trivial. Then turn to a different page and do the same thing. Assign each word to a letter of the alphabet, going in order starting with "a." Implant in your mind an appropriate mental link between each word and your alphabet peg. Write the words down as you go along. See how many you can learn in three minutes. Then, without looking at your list, write down all of the words in some arbitrary order. Make a note of how long it takes you to recall the list. Do this exercise three times. The first time, see how many words you can memorize in three minutes. The second time, see how many you can learn in five minutes, and the third time, see how many you can learn in seven minutes. Then answer the following questions:

1. How many words were you able to memorize in three minutes? Five minutes? Seven minutes?
2. How many words were you able to recall correctly each time?
3. How long did it take you to recall each list?

EXERCISE 7:   Repeat Exercise 6, but this time do not write down the words. You may, however, write down the letters of the alphabet during recall.

Now take your *left* arm, stretch it over your *right* shoulder, and give yourself a big pat on the back. You're doing great!

BREAK POINT

APPLICATION: REMEMBERING A "TO DO" LIST

Like the Link System and the Number Rhyme System, the Alphabet System can also be used to remember a "to do" list. You can remember a list of 26 chores with just your basic alphabet pegs, and you can recall any chore from the list in any order, even if you've forgotten some of them.

Also, as discussed before, you can either include the "action" word or phrase in your fanciful image or you can disregard it. When doing the exercises, however, practice using the action words.

EXERCISE 8: Memorize the following list of things to do in two minutes using the Alphabet System. Then cover up the list and recall it in order in one minute. Then, covering up the previous lists, write the list in reverse order in your notebook in one minute; finally, recall the list in any random order in one minute (also without peeking!).

Chores to Do	In Order	Reverse Order	Random Order
Pack for a trip			
Read the newspaper			
Set the clock for six			
Go to bed by ten			
Turn on the answering machine			
Call for a taxi			
Pick up a magazine			
Meet for lunch at the coffee shop			
Plan for next weekend			
Call your secretary			
Cancel your doctor's appointment			
Write a speech			
Make a dinner reservation			
Meditate			
Do your exercises			
Call your sister			
Buy a card for your friend			

Chores to Do	In Order	Reverse Order	Random Order

Pick up a
  schedule at
  the airline

Decide whether
  to hire the
  new person

Listen to an
  audiotape

Call your
  accountant

Take out your
  contact lenses

Send your suit
  to the cleaners

Iron your tie

Change socks

Practice your
  memory
  techniques

APPLICATION: REMEMBERING HOW TO SPELL TROUBLESOME WORDS

The Alphabet System can also be used to remember how to spell certain troublesome words or to choose the correct word when two words are similar. For example, suppose you often confuse the word "principal" (as in "a principal of the company" or "the school principal") with the word "principle" (as in "the first principle of marketing" or "he has high principles"). You could associate the alphabet peg "ape" with "principal" (which has the letter "a") and form a mental image of an **ape** as the **principal** of your company or school. With that ridiculous image in mind you will always remember that "the principal is an ape" and so the other word must be "principle."

    Here are a few additional examples:

Advice	The noun, as in "good advice," has the letter "c." You can associate it with the alphabet peg word **sea** as in "a **sea** of **advice**." Then you will also automatically remember the verb "advise," as in "Please advise me."

Affect	This verb, as in "It affects me," has the letter "a." Associate it with **ape** as in "You **affect** me when you **ape** around." Then you will automatically remember the other word, "effect," as in "Look at the effect."
Cemetery	Spelled with an "e" after the "t," not an "a." Think of a "dead **eel** in the **cemetery**" (who shocked himself to death?).
Dessert	With the calories, as in "chocolate dessert," has a double "s." Think of two **Eskimos** eating whale blubber (fat!) for **dessert.** Then you will remember the other word is spelled "desert" as in "a dry desert island" or "he deserted his post."
Embarrass	has a *pair* of "r's" (not just one), just as everything else on the **ark** (and aren't all those animals **embarrassed** about being naked together?)
Pursue	The second letter is "u," not "e." Think of a U-boat that **pursues** its quarry.
Their	Refers to something owned by other people, as opposed to "there," which refers to a place. For example, "It is their money" and "there is the money." Since **their** has the letter "i," you can link it with the alphabet peg word **eye,** which *people* have.

EXERCISE 9:   Here is a list of some frequently misspelled or confused words. Following the samples above, for each one think up a mental link based on your alphabet pegs that would help you to remember the correct spelling.

Word	Link
Accommodate	
Choose/chose	
Commitment	
Conscience/conscious	
Conscientious	
Consensus	
Council/counsel	
Disappoint	
Exaggerate	
License	
Occurred	

Word	Link

Omitted
Parallel
Personal/personnel
Possess
Precede/proceed
Rhythm
Stationary/stationery
To/too/two

EXERCISE 10:   Make a list of some words whose spelling gives you trouble. Then use your alphabet pegs to write down next to each a mental link that will help you to remember the correct spelling. Study what you've written. Put the list in some obvious place, such as over your desk. Practice recalling the words and their links three or four times a day over the course of this program. And, of course, add to the list as you think of more words!

From now on you can use the Alphabet System to remember a list of things or activities, just as you can use the Link System and the Number Rhyme System (with differences that we will discuss later). You can also use the Alphabet System to help you remember letter patterns, such as in the spelling of certain troublesome words.

As mentioned earlier, *all* of these memory systems have distinct advantages and disadvantages. Keep in mind that you need to maintain your skill level in all of these methods to get the most from your natural memory power.

DAY 5

REVIEW AND PRACTICE

Over these first few days of this program you've learned some basic essentials:

- Basic principles of memory power
- How to create mental links
- How to create and use memory pegs
- How to apply some specific techniques to memorizing a list of things, a to-do list, and correct spelling.

In addition, you established a personal bench mark of your memory ability at the start of this program, which, as you have no doubt already suspected, is being far surpassed by your rapidly growing abilities!

Now we'll take some time out to review the specific things we've covered and to do some additional practice exercises.

We've agreed to treat memory as a skill. That means we work at it in much the same way as we might work at learning to play tennis or the piano, or to speak a foreign language. And that also means that such things as age, intelligence, or educational background are not significant factors.

The Basic Memory Principles of association, imagination and organization are the building blocks for all of the memory techniques. Association refers to the way we can understand new information by making it relate in some way to something we already know. Imagination helps us to do this, by involving many of our senses and by turning ordinary information into something extraordinary, and hence more memorable. And organization refers to the systematic way we go about using our memory abilities.

The idea behind the Link System is to use the Basic Memory Principles to create a mental link between something you already know, such as an item in a list of things, and something you do not yet know, such as the next item in the list. The more you can employ the memory principles, especially those of imagination, the easier it will be to implant a strong mental link in your mind.

The Number Rhyme System and the Alphabet System rely on memory peg words, which you must first create and learn. You must learn these pegs so well that you can recite them as quickly as you can your name and address. These pegs should be yours, personally, for them to be most effective. And of course each time you make use of these pegs you are automatically learning them even better.

The Number Rhyme System makes use of something with which you are already familiar and comfortable, the whole numbers one through ten. Perhaps you even recall the children's rhyme:

> One, two, buckle your shoe,
> Three, four, close the door,
> Five, six, pick up sticks,
> Seven, eight, close the gate,
> Nine, ten, say it again.

So the idea of a word that rhymes with a number word is not so strange.

In similar fashion, the Alphabet System makes use of the alphabet, which is already well ingrained in your memory and experience. Instead of finding a rhyming word for each letter, however, we need only find a word that starts with the same sound. This is actually much easier, aside from being much more practical. Imagine, for example, using the word "ski" as a peg for the letter "b"—it could not work because "ski" also rhymes with the letter "c" and the letter "d" and the letter "e" and so on. But the word "bee" sounds exactly like the letter "b" and it's so nice and short, concrete, and vivid as well!

Once you have your peg words for the Number Rhyme and Alphabet systems, you employ the technique of linking to associate the word or task you are trying to remember with the peg word. So the Number Rhyme System and the Alphabet System rely on the Link System, and the Link System in turn relies on the Basic Memory Principles.

Each of the three memory systems we've looked at so far, the Link System, the Number Rhyme System, and the Alphabet System, has distinct advantages and disadvantages. An important advantage of the Link

System, for instance, is that it makes use of the basic skill of linking, which is necessary for the other two systems (as well as for other techniques we will look at later). So by using the Link System on a regular basis you'll be practicing the valuable skill of linking.

Another advantage of using the Link System is that there is no limit to the number of items you can commit to memory. Unlike the peg systems (the Number Rhyme System is a type of peg system), the Link System doesn't limit you to a set of existing pegs or force you to create new ones.

A disadvantage of the Link System, however, is that you must recall the items in proper order, for if you start to try recalling them out of order you break your links. The strength of the Link System is that by knowing one item you will automatically know the next. But of course if you forget one item then you have broken the chain and may therefore not be able to recall any items that follow.

With the peg systems you can actually forget one or more items and still recall the rest with ease. You probably already experienced that while doing the exercises. As long as you don't allow yourself to get nervous about forgetting an item or two, you can just continue recalling the other items with ease and confidence.

The peg systems are of course limited by the sets of pegs that you must create and learn in advance. In practical terms, however, you may rarely have need for more than the 26 pegs of the Alphabet System, or even 20 or 10 pegs of the Number Rhyme System.

As you've already discovered during the exercises, the Number Rhyme System allows fairly easy recall of items in particular positions in your list (for example, the twelfth item). That feat would be a bit more difficult with the Alphabet System. On the other hand, the Alphabet System offers a basic set of 26 pegs without requiring a special descriptor to extend the basic set, as does the Number Rhyme System. And of course you can use the Alphabet System to solve other memory problems, such as spelling. (Later you will see how the Number Rhyme System can be applied to certain situations involving numbers.)

The bottom line is that all three techniques have value. You are therefore *strongly urged* to continue to develop your skill with all three techniques. To this end, here is a power exercise.

EXERCISE 1: The purpose of this exercise is to build memory power and to demonstrate how much you can actually remember using the three techniques you've learned and practiced. Do each step without taking any breaks.

Step 1: As quickly as you can, memorize this list of 20 items, using the Link System.

List #1

Ice cream	Pencil
Mountain	Cigar
Pump	Flashlight
Chair	Soft
Mirror	Roach
Sweetness	Hearse
Tennis racquet	Folder
Cucumber	Menu
Monkey	Garbage
Pillow	Staircase

Step 2: As quickly as you can, memorize this list of 20 items, using the Number Rhyme System (do *not* write down numbers next to the words).

List #2

Wealthy	Devious
Rabbit	Hangover
Pizza	Corn
Rocks	TV
Bell	Sewing machine
Toothache	Teacher
Switch	Child
Drawer	Lips
Ceiling	Nephew
Post office	Aggravation

Step 3: As quickly as you can, memorize this list of 26 items using the Alphabet System (do *not* write down letters next to the words).

List #3

Baseball	Supermarket
Knife	Eraser
Table	Trout
Potato	Aspirin
Paper	Sandal
Token	Margarine
Floor	Zipper
Face	Ear
Snake	Snow
Taxi	Rubber band
Wool	Traffic sign
Head	Lamp
Ink	Library

Step 4: As quickly as you can, write down in your notebook all of the 66 items from the three lists in proper order.

List #1 + List #2 + List #3

Congratulations! You have just memorized 66 items! Now, take a break before continuing.

BREAK POINT

Now that you've had a 10- or 15-minute break, do the following exercise.

EXERCISE 2: Write down again, as quickly as you can and in proper order, all of the 66 items you memorized in the previous exercise.

Now, how did you do this time? You'll probably find that you still did pretty well, even though you didn't expect to have to remember those 66 items after recalling them the first time. You might have thought you'd forget them. But the mind stores information very well when you use effective techniques to input the information initially, as happens when you apply the techniques you've been learning in this program.

If you're really ambitious you might try recalling this entire list again tomorrow, or even the next day, just to prove to yourself that you can indeed remember things over the long term, if you want to!

On the other hand, don't be discouraged if you had problems with the list of 66 items. Remember, you've only spent a few days on this memory program—it does take practice to learn new skills! But if you did have problems, do the following exercise.

EXERCISE 3: The purpose of this exercise is to analyze any problems that you may have had with Exercises 1 and 2. Look at your recall list for Exercise 1 and answer these questions:

1. Where did you have trouble recalling words? From the link list, the number rhyme list or the alphabet list? This should tell you where you may need additional practice. If so, go back to the appropriate section, review some of the examples, and redo the exercises there.
2. Did you have difficulty recalling only certain kinds of words, such as the more abstract type? If so, then you need to work on linking abstract words to concrete images. Pick some words from the dictionary and practice linking them to tangible items.
3. Did it seem to take you a very long time to recall the list? If so, then you need to work on speed. Look back at the exercises presented for each technique that work on speed using the dictionary. Try them again.

Now answer the same questions for your recall list of Exercise 2. When you are finished, answer these additional questions:

4. How many words did you fail to recall in Exercise 2 that you *were* able to recall in Exercise 1? Try to figure out why. Perhaps your original mental images for those words were not very vivid, or absurd, etc., and so the links would tend to fade quickly. If this is the case, then you should review the Basic Memory Principles and practice using them to create *strong* mental images.

5. Did you find yourself feeling fatigued? This often happens when focusing hard for a longer period than one is used to. The cure, again, is practice. Work on memorizing increasingly longer lists while noting how long you can maintain your concentration. It should improve with practice. Don't forget to give yourself a break every so often!

One closing comment. You may be wondering why we spent so much time on list learning. The answer is that lists form the basis of much of what we have to learn. Sometimes it's a list of items to buy, other times it's a list of tasks, or a list of dates, or a list of phone numbers, or a list of appointments, or a list of new words. As you'll see over the course of this program, list learning is a vital skill for many memory situations.

DAY 6

TECHNIQUE: THE ROMAN ROOM SYSTEM (LOCI METHOD)

The Roman Room System, also called the Loci Method, is probably the oldest memory technique still used today. The ancient Romans used it to memorize speeches that sometimes lasted several hours.

The technique is essentially another type of peg system. Again, once you've chosen your pegs and learned them well, you can associate each item you wish to remember with one of your pegs.

As with the previous techniques we looked at, you can use this technique to remember all kinds of lists. But it is also effective for remembering simple speeches, stories or jokes.

The pegs you will use with this technique are the items or places in your home. And you use them sequentially. That is, you keep them in the same order as you would encounter them upon entering your home. So the first peg might be your front door; the second might be a coat rack in your entrance hall; the third might be a hallway closet; the fourth might be the fireplace mantel in your living room, and so on.

Incidentally, the word "loci" is plural for the word "locus," which means "place." The "c" in loci is soft, and so it's pronounced like an "s." The word is of Latin origin.

There are several advantages to using places or items in your home as memory pegs. Since you are already intimately familiar with them it should be easy to memorize them. Also, the comfort you will feel with these familiar memory pegs is a refreshing contrast to the discomfort most people feel when giving a speech. In a moment of "stage fright," for example, you need only close your eyes and visualize your home. This will help get you back properly anchored to the job at hand.

Now to select your loci. First you will sketch a picture of your home. You might also include the surrounding areas, such as a front or back yard, a garage, the building's entrance if an apartment, etc. Then you will list, in proper order, the loci you will use as memory pegs. Finally, you will commit the list to memory.

EXERCISE 1: Sketch a picture of your home in your notebook. Don't try to be a good artist; do try to be complete. Take your time but go through your home in a particular direction (e.g., clockwise) that would be natural to follow. You might imagine you are giving someone a tour. Be sure not to pick items that are moved from place to place nor items that are new and not yet familiar to you. You can, however, include things which would be part of your "dream home"—such as a sauna in your bedroom closet—as long as the image is very strong. Also, do not pick the same type of item more than once, such as a doorknob (unless it's a very unique one!). Aim for at least 30 places or items.

EXERCISE 2: Now take yourself on a mental tour of your home following the sketch you just made. As you do so, write down in your notebook the 30 most memorable places or items. Be sure they are in a particular (i.e., the most natural) order. These will be your loci pegs.

Loci Peg #	Item/Place
1	
2	
3	
4	
5	
etc.	

EXERCISE 3: Spend several minutes studying your list of 30 loci pegs. Visualize each one carefully until you have a strong, familiar image of it in your mind. Replace any that are weak. Each one should naturally and easily lead you to the next. Replace any that do not. Look back at your sketch if you need to.

EXERCISE 4: Commit your list of 30 loci pegs to memory. Close your eyes if it helps. You must be able to visualize and name all of the pegs quickly, easily, and comfortably.

BREAK POINT

APPLICATION: LEARNING A SPEECH

Now we can turn our attention to applying the Roman Room System to learning a speech. The method is simple: First you identify key words in your speech and then link these to your loci pegs, in proper sequence. Then, to deliver the speech, you need only visualize yourself "stepping through" your home, allowing your loci pegs to trigger the key ideas in the speech.

But there are also other important aspects of preparing a speech. And since many of these have an effect on how well you will ultimately remember the speech, it's worth taking some time to examine them.

Probably the first question to deal with is whether you should attempt to memorize the speech word for word. My experience has been that it's not a good idea to do this. Only in cases where each word may be closely analyzed afterward, such as a speech by a world leader, would it make sense to try to deliver a speech word for word. And if it were indeed that critical then reading the speech would be the best approach.

It most cases, however, the purpose of the speech maker is to deliver a message or a set of ideas. What particular words the speaker uses to express these ideas is far less important than the ideas themselves. So memorizing *ideas* rather than *words* should be your goal.

Also, a speech that has been memorized word for word can sound stale or phony if it's too polished. There ought to be some spontaneity in the speaker's voice and mannerisms; this helps maintain audience interest. It also helps the audience remember what you've said. And that should be one of your main objectives.

Below is a suggested list of steps to follow in preparing a speech. Over the years, I've found that by following these steps you can make the actual delivery of the speech or presentation easier, more interesting for the audience, and more fun for you.

1. **Know your audience.**   Find out who the audience is, why they are there and what they are interested in hearing about. For example, a group of teachers who have been told by the school principal that they are required to attend your talk on "Reading Readiness in Kindergarten" will have a very different interest level than a group of teachers who have each paid $150 of their own money to attend your seminar on "How to Earn Extra Income as a Part-Time Reading Consultant."

   If you have a clear image in your mind of the audience and

their interests, you can use that image while delivering the speech to help keep yourself riveted to your purpose.

2. **Decide what result you would like to achieve.**   What would you like the audience to do as a result of your speech? For example, do you want the audience to take some action, such as buy your book or sign a petition? Or do you want to entertain them? Each speech should have a very definite purpose. Have that purpose clearly implanted in your mind prior to and throughout your speech. It will help keep you moving through your material.

3. **Decide what you want to communicate.**   Not what you want to *say*, which has to do with the words you use, but what *ideas* you wish to pass on to your audience. Write these out in short sentences or words as they occur to you, without trying to organize them in any way. Include everything, even if you think it irrelevant at first.

4. **Organize your ideas into categories or main ideas.**   Now organize your ideas under general headings. Don't yet try to put them in sequential order, just group them under some logical main ideas. Ask yourself whether these ideas are compatible with the audience's interests and with your objectives.

You should always be able to reconstruct your speech as long as you have a clear image of the main ideas you want to convey.

5. **Decide what visual aids you will need.**   Sometimes you can communicate your ideas more effectively by showing slides than by verbal description. Speakers can forget that an audience often pays closer attention to what they see than to what they hear. If you have any doubts just ask yourself this question: Which are more people hooked on, television or radio?

Visuals can also serve as a memory aid for you, the speaker. I know many executives who regularly plan their entire speech around a slide show. They use each slide as a memory peg: They put up the slide and then talk about it. Of course you must plan this out carefully in advance.

6. **Decide what mood or tone you would like to set.**   Do you want to appear sincere? Diplomatic? Angry? Some of my professional colleagues believe that the mood you project, through your body language, voice, tone and pacing, has more of an impact on the audience than the actual words you use. Decide on how you want to "come across" and plant that image firmly in your mind. In the event that you forget *what* you want to say, you can always make

something up on the basis of the *mood* you want to project.

7. **Sketch the speech.**   Lay out your speech by organizing your main ideas into a logical sequence. Then add some details (subideas) under each main idea. You can write out the speech word for word, even if you don't plan to deliver it that way, if you feel it will help you learn the material better. Otherwise, just write out short statements under each of your main ideas. Either way, try to follow these guidelines:

   • Don't try to say too much at once. One paragraph for one idea or point. Pause between points.
   • Use simple language whenever possible. Avoid unnecessary adjectives.
   • Vary your language and sentence structure. Also plan to vary your pacing and voice intonation.
   • Plan to talk directly to individuals in the audience. Make eye contact. Don't make the mistake of visualizing a sea of nondescript faces.

8. **Apply the Roman Room System to the text of your speech.**   Now we come to the point where you can use your loci pegs. Go through the text of your speech—whether you've written it out word for word or only sketched it doesn't matter—and circle or underline or color code the *key words* that will trigger the idea or point you want to communicate. The ideal would be one key word for each point. Then use linking to mentally associate each of your key words, in proper sequence, to one of your loci pegs. (An example follows shortly.)

   For detailed elaboration of a particular idea you could use subloci. For example, if your bedroom closet were one locus you could also designate its contents, such as the hangers, the shoe rack, and the tie rack, as three subloci that you can use as pegs for further detail or elaboration.

9. **Rehearse your speech using your loci pegs.**   Now practice the speech using only your loci pegs as a memory aid. Imagine taking your audience on a "tour of your ideas" as you "step through" your loci. Practice out loud. Record it and listen to yourself. Get a feel for the proper pacing. For example, you might plan to use a loci peg for each half-minute you speak. That of course would mean one new idea for each half-minute. And this would also help you to organize and keep track of your time when delivering the speech.

Now here's an example of how to use the loci pegs. Suppose the first four ideas in your speech are

Rising costs
Narrowing profit margins
Increased competition
Shortage of qualified labor

And also suppose that your first four loci pegs are

Asphalt driveway
Garage
Backdoor
Kitchen

Here, then, are the links you might use:

Loci pegs	Links
1. asphalt driveway	Imagine that your **asphalt driveway** is really made of gold (**costs**), and that it's **rising** (like a cake in the oven).
2. garage	Picture the walls of your **garage**, papered in dollar bills (**profits**), closing in (**narrowing**).
3. backdoor	See a vision of millions of your **competitors** pouring into your home through the **backdoor**.
4. kitchen	Imagine entering your **kitchen** and finding **no one qualified** even to boil water!

Will you confuse the first two and think of "rising profits" and "narrowing costs"? I don't think so, not if you know what you're talking about! Remember, these memory techniques are just *triggers* for what you already know, what is already stored in your mind.

Also, let me point out once again that it's harder to explain these mental links on paper than it is actually to create them in the mind. Take a moment and really try to see these images.

EXERCISE 5: Here's an exercise to practice applying your loci pegs. Below are some excerpts of a history-making speech delivered by Mikhail Gorbachev, the Soviet General Secretary, to the United Nations on December 7, 1988. Pretend *you* have to deliver these remarks. It should take about two minutes. Apply your loci pegs and then deliver the speech to a friend, your mirror, or your tape recorder. Afterward, read through the speech again to see how much of it you were able to memorize.

The world in which we live today is radically different from what it was at the beginning or even in the middle of this century. And it continues to change as do all its components. The advent of nuclear weapons was just another tragic reminder of the fundamental nature of that change. A material symbol and expression of absolute military power, nuclear weapons at the same time revealed the absolute limits of that power.

The problem of mankind's survival and self-preservation came to the fore.

It is obvious, for instance, that the use or threat of force no longer can or must be an instrument of foreign policy. This applies above all to nuclear arms, but that is not the only thing that matters. All of us, and primarily the stronger of us, must exercise self-restraint and totally rule out any outward-oriented use of force.

That is the first and the most important component of a nonviolent world as an ideal which we proclaimed together with India in the Delhi Declaration and which we invite you to follow.

The new phase also requires de-ideologizing relations among states. We are not abandoning our convictions, our philosophy, or traditions, nor do we urge anyone to abandon theirs.

But neither do we have any intention to be hemmed in by our values. That would result in intellectual impoverishment, for it would mean rejecting a powerful source of development—the exchange of everything original that each nation has independently created.

In the course of such exchange, let everyone show the advantages of their social system, way of life or values—and not just by words or propaganda, but by real deeds.

We regard prospects for the near and more distant future quite optimistically.

Just look at the changes in our relations with the United States. Little by little, mutual understanding has started to develop and elements of trust have emerged, without which it is very hard to make headway in politics.

I am convinced that our time and the realities of today's world call for internationalizing dialogue and the negotiating process. This is the main, the most general conclusion that we have come to in studying global trends that have been gaining momentum in recent years, and in participating in world politics.

BREAK POINT

APPLICATION: REMEMBERING A JOKE OR STORY

Learning a joke or story is similar to learning a speech. The only real difference is that if you are *hearing* the joke or story you don't have the opportunity to identify the key words at your leisure. You've got to pick out key words and assign them to your loci pegs as you are listening. And that can be a bit tricky because you don't have the time to analyze and think about what information is important. You also don't know where the story is going, or what the punch line of the joke is.

Let's take an example which simulates (as best as we can in written form) your hearing a story.

EXERCISE 6:   Read through the following story only once without stopping to analyze or think about what you are reading. As you read, underline or circle what you believe to be the key words.

God once asked a group of men if they knew what death meant. The men said that they did not. God, wanting to teach them the meaning of death, asked them to come back at six o'clock in the evening. When they arrived, God asked them once again if they knew what death meant, and again they said they did not. God told them to remain standing for a while. At eight o'clock He asked them once again, and once again got the same answer. However, the men were beginning to grow tired of standing around and waiting, and by ten o'clock they had all fallen asleep. God then woke them and said;

"So, now you know the meaning of death, for it is just like sleep!"

(Adapted from an ancient African tale)

This is an easy story to remember if you can identify the key words that trigger the main points when hearing it only once. Afterward, of course, it is easier to identify the key words by going back and reading the story again.

EXERCISE 7: Link the key words from the story in the previous exercise to your loci pegs. Then, without peeking, retell the story out loud.

Suppose you identified these key words: God, men, death, waiting, sleep. You can memorize these key words by linking them to your first five loci pegs. It might look something like this:

1. Front door	**God**'s heavenly door to paradise
2. Hallway closet	Filled with hordes of **men**
3. Fireplace mantle	**Death**—An urn filled with ashes of cremation
4. Fireplace	Logs **waiting** eagerly to be lit (they are gasping with anticipation)
5. Hearth rug	The rug, formerly alive, is now **sleeping** (let sleeping rugs lie?)

EXERCISE 8: Learn the following in the same way as you did in the previous two exercises. But this time don't pause after identifying the key words or phrases. Go through the material just once, identifying the key words and immediately linking them to your loci pegs. Then cover the text and recount the story.

Samuel, a tailor, came to America from a small town in Russia, not knowing how to read or write English. Still he was able to open a shop and began to do well. Soon he needed to open a bank account, so he went to the bank and, unable to write, signed his name by making two crosses.

He continued to prosper as the years passed. He sold his small tailor shop, went into the retail business and then into manufacturing. Soon he needed to go to the bank again, to open a new account for his expanding business. This time, however, instead of marking his name with two crosses he used three.

"Why three crosses instead of the usual two?" asked the bank manager.

"Oh that," said Samuel, "my wife got so carried away with my success she insists I should take on a middle name!" (Jewish folk tale)

You can now use the Roman Room System to remember simple stories or jokes which you read or hear. You can also use it, just as the ancient Roman orators did, to memorize speeches.

For long speeches or stories you may find that you need more than 30 loci pegs. Or you may want to create subloci for detailed subideas. In any case, the key to becoming skilled at this technique, as always, is practice. So look for opportunities to use this technique—perhaps when you've got to give a speech, or the next time you're listening to your favorite comedian or storyteller.

EXERCISE 9: The purpose of this exercise is to build speed and power with the Roman Room System. Begin immediately to apply it to stories you read or speeches you hear. (Follow the instructions for the previous exercise.) Use stories you read in newspapers or magazines, and presentations you hear on radio or television or at work. Practice using the technique in this way at least four times in the next 24 hours.

DAY 7

TECHNIQUE: MIND MAPPING (CLUSTERING)

APPLICATION: REMEMBERING WHAT YOU'VE READ

APPLICATION: REMEMBERING WHAT YOU'VE HEARD

APPLICATION: PREPARING FOR AN EXAM OR PRESENTATION

When it comes to learning complex material you may find the Roman Room System not the best technique. That's because it's a linear technique. In other words, it deals with information from beginning to end in a straightforward, step-by-step way. While this may be fine for simple speeches, stories, and jokes, it becomes difficult to use with more complex material such as that presented in a lecture, textbook, or report, or when you are preparing for an exam or complex presentation.

As an example, think of how most textbooks are organized. First there's the title. This usually defines the main subject, such as *European History: 1900–1946*. Then there are different chapters, each of which is a subtopic of the main topic. So one chapter might be called "The Early Years" and another might be called "The Middle Years" and another "The Later Years." And each chapter might be broken down into geographic areas, such as "Eastern Europe," "Great Britain," "Western Europe," and so on. And then each of these areas might be further subdivided. Then, too, there would be discussions of the relationships among these different areas during different periods of time, such as treaties or wars between certain countries.

Now, isn't real life more complex than a simple story or joke? No matter how hard a textbook writer may try to organize the information in a nice orderly fashion, human events don't really take place in a step-by-step sequence without being connected to something else in some other place or at some other time. And that's true for history, economics, business, psychology, and science.

To learn and remember complex information properly (where there are subtopics and relationships among the subtopics) we need a new technique.

The technique called Mind Mapping, or Clustering, is a good technique for such material. It's more graphic than the other techniques we've looked at; that is, it will make more use of your ability to visualize the way key words are organized on paper than the way you remember hearing them.

The basic idea is to take the key words and graphically "map them out" according to their relationships to one another. So you would put the main idea in the center and the subideas as branches from the main idea. Then put in the smaller subideas as smaller branches, etc. Connections between subideas are easily marked just by drawing lines between them.

Suppose you had to write a paper, or give a presentation, on the weather. Of course many ideas come to mind. But instead of just writing them down in any haphazard way, let's use Mind Mapping to organize the information as we think of it. On the next page is one way it might look when you're done.

Notice that the main idea, "The Weather," is in the center, and the immediate subtopics are branches from the main idea. The smaller subtopics are smaller branches.

One of the reasons this technique is so effective is that it makes use of the way the human brain actually works. Unfortunately (or fortunately), our minds don't work in a nice linear fashion, especially when we are creating ideas. Rather, we tend to roam all over, thinking of different things almost at the same time. And we quickly see how different things may be related.

This technique of clustering makes it easy to write down your thoughts, without forcing you to be logical and sequential. You can even use pictures or symbols instead of words. You can always reorganize the information later if it needs to be in a more sequential or logical order.

The same principles operate when we read or listen to information that's more than just a simple narrative, such as a passage in a textbook, a lengthy lecture, or a complex business presentation. Mind Mapping can be especially helpful in these cases, for it is a well-established fact that we forget much of what we have heard or read soon afterward. Some

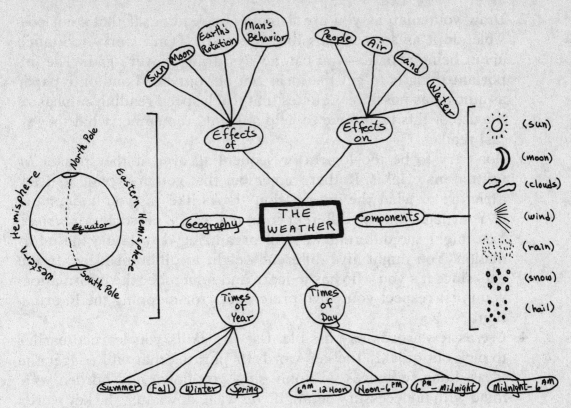

estimates, for example, are that we forget 80 percent of what we've read within 8 hours!

Another reason Mind Mapping is effective is that it makes use of the mind's spatial abilities. Conclusions from left brain/right brain research suggest that the left side of the human brain is responsible for verbal skills while the right side deals with spatial skills. So you could say that this technique makes use of your entire brain!

You might not feel entirely comfortable with this technique in the beginning. That is probably because it's new to you. After all, most of us were taught to make linear outlines or summaries, from top to bottom, in nice logical sequence. This technique, however, is more "free form." It gives you permission to be more flexible with your thoughts and associations.

Here are some tips for using Mind Mapping effectively:

1. Give yourself plenty of paper, especially if you don't know how much information you're going to have to process. You don't want to find yourself suddenly having to write along the edges of the page! Also, you might feel more comfortable with the paper held sideways.

2. Draw your map as you are listening or reading. If that's not possible, do it as soon as possible afterward. Don't worry too much about being artistic—you can always draw it over again. The important thing is to get the ideas out of your head and onto paper as quickly as possible. Courses that teach speed reading emphasize the use of this technique to help students remember what they've just read.

3. Don't try to be too logical or sequential, even if the speaker or written material is. Rather, remember that you are trying to draw a picture of what the information "looks like" as you understand it. Your logic may be different from that of the presenter or writer. You might see different ways of organizing or relating the information. You might give different weight to different ideas. In the end, since it's you who has to learn and remember the information, you must respect your own preferences for mapping the information!

4. Use as few words as possible. Use the skills you learned earlier to pick out quickly the key words or phrases that will trigger the ideas. Long sentences will only slow you down and burden your mind with unnecessary detail. If you write down just the key words and then think about them as you listen or read, they'll have meaning for you later.

5. Go from the general to the specific whenever possible. This should be easy, for if the material is presented well it should also be organized in this way. Your resulting mind map will then have general ideas nearer the center and specifics as you move away from the center.

6. Know your purpose before you begin reading or listening. As mentioned earlier in connection with preparing a speech, it helps to know what you're aiming for. In this case, you should be able to answer questions such as these: "What do I want to find out?" What am I looking for?" "What am I listening for?" "How does this relate to me?"

7. If possible, read or listen to the material twice. If you've tape-recorded a presentation, for example, you can just play it back a second time. If so, you can use the second go-round to add more detail to your map, or make new cross-connections, or combine two related ideas, or separate a big idea into several smaller ideas.

8. One method you might use to organize your map is by certain familiar words. For example, with the main idea at the center you

might label eight more branches as follows: WHO, WHAT, WHEN, WHERE, WHY, HOW, HOW MUCH, RESULT. Then, as you listen or read you can just answer these questions by extending your map from each of them.

9. When you've finished your map, sit back and study it. Try to see it graphically as well as verbally. That is, try to let your brain see the layout, the branches, and the relationships. You'll be surprised how well your mind can make use of this visual input to recall the information later. Try to make sense of the information, not as separate chunks but as all the parts are related to each other and to the main idea.

BREAK POINT

EXERCISE 1: Review the mind mapping tips above. Then read the following excerpt from *How to Settle an Estate or Prepare Your Will*,* drawing a map as you go along. Read the material a second time and refine or redraw your map. When you are done, study your map. Then, without referring back to the original passage or your map, recall as much of the material as possible. Check back to see how well you did. Then pretend you've got to present the material to an audience: Recall it out loud in front of your mirror, or to a friend or into a tape recorder.

Choosing an Administrator and Attorney

If a person dies intestate [without leaving a will], the court will appoint an administrator to settle the estate. Often this person is a family member or a close business associate. Normally, someone will volunteer, and the court will appoint whomever it considers the best person for the job. The court will give the administrator a certificate or "letter of administration" (if there is a will this is called a "letter testamentary"), which states the administrator has

---

*Toni P. Lester (New York: Perigee Books), pp. 27–28. Reprinted by permission.

authority to settle the estate. This is a valuable piece of paper, since it enables the administrator to withdraw funds from the deceased person's bank accounts, receive stock dividends, and generally do whatever must be done to take possession of estate assets.

After the administrator has the estate appraised, he or she should file the appropriate federal and state tax returns as soon as possible. Once all taxes and claims have been paid, the administrator can petition the court to be allowed to distribute estate assets to the decedent's heirs. Although the general rule is that the heirs get what's left of the estate only when all other claims have been settled, sometimes probate courts will allow an administrator to give the decedent's family a hardship allowance to cover necessary living expenses during lengthy probate proceedings.

Sometimes the decedent may have a business that must either be sold or be kept operating. The administrator is responsible for doing this too. However, the administrator can hire a professional business manager to operate or wind up the business on his or her behalf. If you do need to hire a manager, make sure you have an experienced attorney draw up a professional services contract for you and the manager to sign. Among other things, the contract should stipulate that no major decisions or actions affecting the business can be taken without your written consent.

It will also probably be necessary for you to hire an attorney to help you settle the estate. Although, theoretically, you can do this yourself, the probate process, with all of its notification and procedural requirements, is often very time-consuming and complicated. Since an estate attorney will know the local probate requirements, you can save yourself the hassle of keeping abreast of all of these things yourself.

Attorneys are usually paid out of the probatable estate. Many states establish what percentage of the estate is payable to the attorney. If you think this amount is too high, try to negotiate an acceptable fee with your attorney. Sometimes the lawyer will accept an hourly rate, which may result in lower fees. Whatever you agree to, make sure you have discussed fees and are satisfied with the fee arrangement before signing any contracts to retain the attorney as your representative.

There, you've learned some new material, organized it, and then presented it from memory!

EXERCISE 2: In this exercise, pretend you are listening to a live presentation of the material below.* Draw a mind map in your notebook as you go along, but do not go back over the original material a second time. This should make it more difficult but also realistic. Then, when done, study your map and memorize the information. Finally, recall the information from memory. Grade yourself on how much of the information you correctly recalled.

Maintaining Eye Contact in an Oral Presentation

If someone looks at you frequently in a private conversation, you feel he or she is interested in you. But if the person looks away, avoiding eye contact, you usually feel uncomfortable—as if you're being excluded.

Similarly, maintaining eye contact is essential to keep an audience actively interested. Techniques for maintaining eye contact may vary with the size of your audience.

For an audience of one, simply look at that person as often as you can. This tends to be a bit difficult when you're reading from a paper, because you have to keep looking down at your notes, thus breaking contact.

That's why rehearsal is so important. The more familiar you become with your written presentation, the more secure you'll feel about looking up from the printed page and speaking directly to your listener.

To remind yourself to maintain eye contact, write a symbol such as an eye, or make a note as "LOOK UP" in the margin of your presentation. Try to do this at least once for every five or six lines of your presentation.

Also, always make eye contact when you're asking a question. This makes the audience feel that you are really expecting them to think about an answer.

If you're speaking to a relatively small audience, say, up to fifteen or twenty people, try to look at all of them periodically. If you're all seated at a large conference table, scan everybody from time to time. Sometimes you might look only to those on your left, sometimes only to the right, and sometimes you'll sweep both left and right.

---

*Lassor A. Blumenthal, *Successful Oral and Written Presentations* (New York: Perigee Books), pp. 62–63. Reprinted with permission.

Many listeners tend to be touchy about this: if they sense you're looking at others but not them, they'll feel you think they're not worthy of attention, and they'll be resentful. You can prevent this simply by remembering to look at everyone.

One political note: Often when you're making a presentation to a small group, one member of the audience will be more important than the others—it may be the boss, or the senior delegate, or simply the one who carries the most influence. Make eye contact with that person more than with the others. This will usually earn his or her good will for two reasons: it shows that you respect the person's seniority, and confirms his or her importance to the rest of the audience.

When you're speaking to larger groups, say, more than twenty-five people, it's difficult to maintain eye contact with everyone. You'll usually find that a large number of people will not be looking at you. This doesn't necessarily mean they're not interested in what you're saying, but it can be discouraging if you interpret it that way.

The solution is to scan the audience until you find two or three or four people in different parts of the room who *are* looking at you with interest. Then, as you speak, talk directly to them, first to one, then to another. This will help you feel that you're making person-to-person contact. Consequently, it will strengthen the conviction and persuasiveness of everything you say.

From now on, you can use Mind Mapping to organize information, on the spot, that you must learn. The technique works well, whether you are reading or listening, and is particularly effective with complex material.

How well you organize your maps will depend greatly on how well you make use of the Basic Memory Principles of organization. And once you've organized the information in a way which is meaningful to *you*, your right brain will make sense of the graphic representation.

With practice, you may begin to feel more comfortable with maps than with linear outlines or summaries. You'll begin to appreciate the flexibility and power of the technique.

EXERCISE 3: The purpose of this exercise is to build speed and power with Mind Mapping. Begin immediately applying it to what you read in newspapers, magazines, and books. Also apply it to what you hear on radio and, television and at work. (Follow the instructions for the previous two exercises.) Be sure to practice using the technique in this way at least four times in the next 24 hours.

DAY 8

TECHNIQUE: WORD SUBSTITUTION

APPLICATION: LEARNING NEW WORDS AND NAMES

Word Substitution is a powerful technique. The idea is simply to replace the mundane with the fanciful, the unfamiliar with the familiar, and the forgettable with the memorable. You can then apply this technique to learning new words as well as the names of new people you meet.

You probably already do this from time to time. For example, when a client of mine told his aged mother he was going to Seattle, she asked, "See who?" I don't think he will easily forget the name of that city in Washington!

My last name is Bienstock. I often meet people who come up to me after a talk or seminar and make some reference to a fellow named Jack. Of course I've heard it countless times in my life, as you might imagine. But for the person hearing my name for the first time, replacing Bienstock with Beanstalk—and the image that goes with it—is an effective use of Word Substitution.

Notice how you need to draw on your imagination skills to create a mental image based on the new word. But that should be an easy task since the new word is one with which you are more comfortable or more familiar. And you've been steadily increasing your ability to create fanciful mental images throughout this program.

Now let's look at some specific examples. Below are some examples of how Word Substitution can be applied for different kinds or words or names. These examples are organized into four different categories, namely words or names that 1) sound like other words or phrases, 2) have another meaning in English, 3) have another meaning in a foreign language, and 4) relate to something or someone else you already know.

1. Word Substitution based on sound

Word: *Sacrilegious,* which means "disrespect or damage to something sacred," sounds like "sack religious," which you can think of as an attack ("sack") on religion. For the correct spelling, you can remember that the first "i" and the "e" in sacrilegious are in reverse position (what a disrespectful thing to do!).

Foreign Word: *Champignons* is French for "mushrooms." You can think of **champions** as in "champion-sized (enormous, prize-winning) mushrooms."

Place Name: *Hawaii* sounds like "How are ye?" Imagine those Hula dancers uttering that phrase while hanging leis around your neck as you arrive!

Person's Name: *Clurman* sounds like "clear man"—think of the invisible man?

2. Word Substitution based on another meaning

Word: Some words are created by combining words, or using prefixes (in front) or suffixes (at the end) that have meaning. For example, **monorail** consists of the prefix "mono" (meaning "one") and the word "rail." Thus, monorail refers to a train that operates on a single rail.

Foreign Word: In Spanish, the word *embarazada* means "embarrassed." But is also means "pregnant." You can form the mental link between the two concepts by thinking of an unmarried young girl who is **embarrassed** about being **pregnant**.

Place Name: *Buffalo,* the city in New York State, can be remembered by linking it with the fantasy of being overrun by millions of wild **buffalo** (the animal).

Person's Name: You can easily remember *Campbell* by imagining a can of soup!

3. Word Substitution based on a meaning in another language

Word: If you are familiar with one or more foreign languages, then you can link a word in English with its foreign language counterpart. For example, the word **sate,** which means "to satisfy or fill," comes from the Latin word *satiare,* which has the same meaning.

Foreign Word: Many words or phrases are similar in different languages. This is often due to common origins, such as Latin. Consider, for example, the phrases *por favor* in Spanish and *per favore* in Italian, both of which mean "please."

Place Name: If you know that *croix* in French means "cross," then you can think of *St. Croix* as meaning "Saint's Cross."

Person's Name: My last name, Bienstock, is short for *Bienenstock,* which in German is composed of two words: *Bienen,* (meaning "bees,") and *Stock,* meaning "stem, trunk, stump." So if you know some German you can remember Bienstock by thinking of a beehive!

4. Word Substitution based on something/someone else you know

Word: If you know that the word **suspect** as a noun refers to someone who is considered to have done something wrong (as in "He is a suspect in the murder"), then you can remember that verb "suspect" means to think of a person as a possible suspect (as in "they suspect him"), and that the adjective "suspect" means something should be looked at as possibly unreliable (as in "The information is suspect").

Foreign Word: In learning a foreign language it's always nice when a verb is conjugated in a regular fashion. This makes it easier to remember, since we just need to remember the word's basic stem and then apply the standard endings. For example, some of the conjugations for the Spanish verb *hablar* (which means "to speak") are *hablo, hablas, habla, hablamos, hablan.*

Place Name: You can remember **Florida,** a city in New York, by associating it with the **Florida** where the oranges grow!

Person's Name: If you meet someone named **Horace** you might think of another person of that name whom you've known for many years. You might attribute some characteristic to this new person to link the two. For example, they might both be elderly and crabby. But be careful not to overgeneralize and blame one for the faults of the other!

EXERCISE 1: Add some words or names of your own to each of the categories above. Use a dictionary or thesaurus to help you.

BREAK POINT

TECHNIQUE: DOMINANT FEATURE (UNIQUENESS)

APPLICATION: MATCHING FACES, NAMES, AND JOBS

A common memory situation arises when you are introduced to someone for the first time, such as at a party or a business meeting. How often have you forgotten a new person's name almost immediately? Well, many people have this problem.

Learning to match names and faces is not really a difficult memory problem. But we're hampered in social or business situations with a bit of nervousness. After all, we're usually introduced to others soon after arriving. We haven't yet had a chance to get comfortable with the new situation or surroundings. However, if you're skilled in using the right memory technique you should be able to conquer this common problem.

The method we'll examine is actually a combination of several techniques, but it depends primarily on your ability to find the dominant or unique feature in the other person's face.

With this approach, you'll be able not only to match names with faces correctly, but also to match the correct occupations or jobs.

You might be thinking, "It's hard enough just to match someone's name to their face; why make it more difficult by including their occupation too?" Well, first of all it doesn't take much more effort to remember a person's occupation, as you'll soon see. If you're going to make the effort to memorize the name and the face with just a bit more effort you can also memorize the occupation.

Also, think about what you typically want to know about a person you've just met. Isn't it what they look like, what their name is, and what they do for a living?

In business situations it's especially important to know what a person's job is—sometimes more important than their name. And this holds true whether that person works for your company, is a close friend of your boss, or is an important client of your company.

There are four basic steps:

1. Identify the dominant or unique feature in the person's face.
2. Apply Word Substitution to the person's name.
3. Construct a mental image to represent the person's job.
4. Combine Steps 1, 2, and 3 in a single mental image.

You should carry out each of the first three steps as independently from one another as possible. So when you first look at the person's face you must truly pick out *the* dominant or unique feature. You can't, for example, pick out the feature that best fits their name or job. The idea is to pick out the feature which you'll be sure to identify again, next time you see the face.

Similarly, your word substitution for the person's name should not be based on what they look like or what they do. The best substitution is the one that comes to mind *first* upon hearing the name. That way you'll be able to conjure up the substitute word next time you hear the person's name, regardless of whether or not you see the person's face.

Your mental image of the person's job or occupation should be independent of the person's face or name. In fact, as we shall see later, you can prepare in advance some mental images for some standard occupations.

Let's now look at each of these steps in more detail.

1. Identify the dominant or unique feature in the person's face.

Perhaps some outstanding feature will be immediately obvious, such as bushy eyebrows, or a hooked nose, or a pointed chin. If not, you'll have to scan the person's face quickly. And if you do, get into the habit of doing it in some organized way, such as from the top down. Consider these areas to examine:

Hair	Look for an unusual style, color, or texture. But be careful, especially with women, not to pick something that might change soon!
Forehead	Is it unusually large or broad? Does it have any unusual birth marks or lines?
Eyes	Also the eyebrows. Look for any unusual aspects, such as shape or color. I once knew someone who had one blue eye and one green.
Nose	Is it unusually long, short, small, or narrow? Or does it have some special shape, perhaps like a ski jump?
Ears	Remember Mr. Spock in the television show *Star Trek*? Very unusual ears can often stand out.
Mouth	The mouth and surrounding area such as cheeks, lips, and teeth might be outstanding features. For example: chubby cheeks, thin lips, perfect teeth.
Chin	Exceptionally pointed or rounded chins will stand out. So will unusual dimples.
Skin	Anything unusual about the skin, such as color, texture, marks, or lines?
General	The overall shape of the face might be unusual. For example, is it exceptionally round, or long? An unusually large head?

EXERCISE 2:   Look quickly at each of the following faces and jot down the dominant or unique feature you see. When you are done with all of them, go back to each one in turn and answer this question: "Is this feature what I truly would first notice again, if I were to see this face sometime in the future?" For any face for which your answer is "No," scan the face using the above tips and change your selection of feature.

feature:

feature:

feature:

feature:

feature:

feature:

2. Apply Word Substitution to the person's name.

We've already spent some time discussing how this works. Now try the following exercise.

EXERCISE 3: For each of the following names write a fanciful substitution in your notebook. Some are already done for you. (Only last names are used for this exercise.) As you write down the substitute word, make sure you conjure up the appropriate image in your mind.

Name	Substitute
Abrams	
Arnold	
Burton	
Borden	
Carson	
Cosby	Funny Black comedian (as in Bill Cosby)
Davis	
Dershowitz	
Epsell	
Elliott	
Flanagan	
Forester	
Graham	
Goodstein	
Harrington	
Hughes	Hues (colors)
Isaacson	
Jackson	
Jacoby	
Kaufman	
Kennedy	
Larson	Arson (or l'arson, making it a bit French)
Lawrence	
McDonald	
Meyerson	
Nellis	
Nichols	Nickels
O'Brien	
Owens	

Name	Substitute
Phillips	
Pearlmutter	
Raymond	
Rosenberg	
Schaeffer	Shaver (or the brand-name fountain pen)
Simmons	
Thompson	
Tucker	
Watson	
Weintraub	

EXERCISE 4: Add 10 more names to the list in the previous exercise. Then, giving yourself no more than three minutes in all, provide a substitute for each of them. Be sure to see the images in your mind as you write them down.

BREAK POINT

---

3. Construct a mental image to represent the person's job.

For this step it's important to be very specific and concrete. Also, you must create your mental image based on something the person actually *does* with his or her *hands*. Even if the person's occupation doesn't actually require using hands, you must convert the activity to hand-based activity. You'll learn how to do this in the exercise below.

Even more, you must create a mental image of the person using her hands *in connection with her face*. In this way, when you eventually combine the first three steps in this method you'll always be able to look at the person's face and identify the job or occupation by *what the person's hands are doing* in your mental image. This also means that in Step 2 (above) you should not involve the person's hands in the word substitution for the name.

You can actually prepare some standard mental images in advance. Then you can just apply them quickly when you need them. For now, don't use any specific part of the face. Just try to imagine a specific *hands* activity on the face in general. (Later, of course, you'll see how to apply the hands activity to the dominant or unique feature of the face.)

EXERCISE 5: Next to each of the following jobs or occupations provide a "hands activity" that is done on the face. The first few are already done for you. As you write, be sure you visualize the mental image clearly and strongly!

Job/Occupation	Hand-Face Activity
Accountant	Writes numbers on his face with a pencil.
Actuary	Shuffles mortality tables on her face.
Baker	Uses a rolling pin on his face.
Banker	Counts out money on her face.
Consultant	
Controller	
Dentist	
Druggist	
Elevator operator	
Engineer	
Factory worker	
Furniture maker	
Garage attendant	
Homemaker	
House painter	
Jeweler	
Judge	
Lawyer	
Messenger	
Musician	
Office assistant	
President	
Secretary	
Stock boy	
Teacher	
Vice president	

EXERCISE 6: Add another ten jobs/occupations to the list in the previous exercise. Then, in three minutes, write in the "activities." Be sure you actually see the hands activities in your mind as you write them.

4. Combine Steps 1, 2, and 3 in a single mental image.

Now it's time to put it all together. Suppose you've just been introduced to Mr. Warren at an office party. You quickly use Word Substitution to think "Warren—'war in.' " As you shake his hand you look at his face and immediately notice that Mr. Warren has extremely *large eyes*. And then you are told that Mr. Warren is the company's *accountant*, which of course triggers the image of his writing numbers on his face with a pencil. Putting it all together you conjure up the following silly fantasy:

> On this face are enormous eyes. There is a war in (Warren) there between the powers of light and the powers of darkness. And his hands are up there keeping score by writing on his eyelids with a pencil (just like an accountant!).

There, you've created a fanciful mental image that enables you to "write" this man's name and occupation on his face. The next time you see his face you'll immediately notice the enormous eyes. That will prompt you to think of the "war" in there and then of his writing the score on his lids. You'll then recall that this is Mr. Warren the accountant!

Okay, I know you're thinking, "I'll never be able to do that!" But you will. Others have done it, and so can anyone. It just takes practice. With practice comes confidence, accuracy, and speed. Don't be turned off by all the written explanation. Once you get the hang of actually doing it you'll quickly see that it's far easier to do than to explain. The mind can work at blazing speed when it knows how!

EXERCISE 7: Spend a few minutes studying the following faces and their matching names and jobs. Then turn the page to where the faces are laid out once again, but in a different order. For each face supply the correct name and occupation.

name: Ms. Saunders
occupation: Teacher

name: Mr. Jackson
occupation: Personnel director

name: Mr. Hershkowitz
occupation: Lawyer

name: Mrs. Flynn
occupation: Vice president

name: Mr. Simpson
occupation: Clerk

name: Ms. Fried
occupation: Secretary

name: Mrs. Angelo
occupation: Buyer

name: Mr. O'Dwyer
occupation: Writer

name:
occupation:

name:
occupation:

name:
occupation:

name:
occupation:

name:
occupation:

name:
occupation:

name:
occupation:

name:
occupation:

EXERCISE 8:   To build power and speed, practice identifying the dominant or unique feature in every face you see, for at least the next 24 hours. This includes everyone you pass on the street, everyone you see in the elevator, everyone you see on television, and so on. Get into the habit of looking carefully at faces!

Similarly, use Word Substitution for every name you hear spoken or see in print. You should be able to practice this at least 20 times within the next 24 hours.

And if you think of any jobs or occupations not included in the previous exercises, immediately create a "hands activity" for them.

DAY 9

REVIEW AND PRACTICE

Congratulations! You're now well beyond the halfway point in this program and have undoubtedly increased your memory power greatly.

You've spent the past few days learning some new techniques and their applications. These are:

- The Roman Room System, which uses fixed memory pegs (loci) from your home. You've applied this technique to memorizing a simple speech, story, or joke. You can also use it for other common memory problems, such as memorizing a list of items or chores.
- Mind Mapping, which relies on your ability to organize information in clusters, as you read or hear it. Because this technique requires you to organize the information according to *your* understanding of it, it is an effective technique for remembering what you hear or read. It can also be used to prepare to take an exam or give a presentation.
- Word Substitution, which is an effective way to learn new words or names. It makes extensive use of your imagination and association skills.
- Dominant Feature, which together with Word Substitution and Linking is a powerful technique for learning and remembering "Who's Who and What Do They Do"—that is, matching faces, names and occupations.

You may find that you like one technique more than another, Or you may find one easier to apply than another. That's okay. Just recognize that each technique has its advantages and disadvantages, and that one technique may be better than another in solving some particular memory problem.

Of course you are the ultimate judge of which technique to use in any particular situation. But before you decide on your favorite technique(s), it's a good idea to become skilled at all of them. So continue to keep an open mind, practice all of them, and hold off your final judgment until you've finished this entire program.

There are some distinct advantages of the Roman Room System. Since the pegs (loci) are already familiar to you, you should be able to use the technique to memorize large amounts of information, just as the ancient Romans did.

On the other hand, the Mind Mapping technique allows you to jot down ideas quickly, and to visualize relationships easily. So it's well suited as a tool for remembering complex information—information having several levels or relationships. A clear disadvantage of this technique, however, is that you cannot add too much detail to your map, or it'll just get out of hand!

You can, of course, use these two techniques together. For example, you might use Mind Mapping as you read, and then use the Roman Room System to memorize the information. Try this in the next exercise.

EXERCISE 1:   Read the following excerpt from a NATO statement on arms control.* As you read, draw a map of the information. When you're done, go back and refine your map. Then use your loci pegs to memorize the information. Finally, present the information as you would a speech. Use a tape recorder or a friend to capture your presentation. Grade yourself on how much of the information you correctly recalled.

The major threat to stability in Europe comes from those weapons systems which are capable of mounting large-scale offensive operations and of seizing and holding territory. These are above all main battle tanks, artillery and armored troop carriers. It is in these very systems that the East has such a massive preponderance. Indeed, the Soviet Union itself possesses more tanks and artillery than all the other members of the Warsaw Pact and the Alliance combined. And they are concentrated in a manner which raises grave concerns about the strategy which they are intended to

*Excerpted from a statement by the foreign ministers of the North Atlantic Treaty Organization (NATO) issued on December 8, 1988, *The New York Times*, December 9, 1988.

support as well as their role in maintaining the division of Europe.

The reductions announced by the Soviet Union are a positive contribution to correcting this situation. They indicate the seriousness with which the conventional imbalances which we have so long highlighted as a key problem in European security are now also addressed by the Soviet Government. We also welcome the declared readiness of the Soviet Union to adjust their force posture. The important thing is now to build on these hopeful developments at the negotiating table in order to correct the large asymmetries that will still remain and to secure a balance at lower levels of forces. For this, it will be necessary to deal with the location, nationality and the state of readiness of forces, as well as their numbers. Our proposals will address these issues in the following specific ways:

We shall propose an overall limit on the total holdings of armaments in Europe. This limit should be substantially lower than existing levels, in the case of tanks close to half.

In our concept of stability, no country should be able to dominate the Continent by force of arms. We shall therefore also propose that no country should be entitled to possess more than a fixed proportion, such as 30 percent, of the total holdings in Europe.

Limiting numbers and nationality of forces would not by itself affect the stationing of forces on other countries' territory. Stationed forces, particularly those in active combat units, are especially relevant to surprise attack. We shall propose limits on such forces.

Our proposal will apply to the whole of Europe. In order to avoid undue concentration of these weapon categories in certain areas of Europe, we shall propose appropriate sub-limits.

To buttress the resulting reductions in force levels in the whole of Europe, we shall propose stabilizing measures. These could include measures of transparency, notifications and constraint applied to the deployment, movement and levels of readiness of conventional armed forces, which include conventional armaments and equipment.

Finally, we shall require a rigorous and reliable regime for monitoring and verification. This would include the periodic exchange of detailed data about forces and deployments, and the right to conduct on-site inspections.

In order to create transparency of military organization, we plan to introduce a proposal for a wide-ranging comprehensive annual exchange of information concerning military organization, manpower and equipment as well as major weapon deployment programs. To evaluate this information we will propose modalities for the establishment of a random evaluation system.

In addition, we will propose measures in such areas as:

More detailed information with regard to the notification of military exercises;

Improvements in the arrangements for observing military activities;

Greater openness and predictability about military activities;

A strengthening of the regime for insuring compliance and verification.

Finally, we shall propose additional measures designed to improve contacts and communications between participating states in the military field; to enhance access for military staffs and media representatives; and to increase mutual understanding of military capabilities, behavior and force postures. We will also propose modalities for an organized exchange of views on military doctrine tied to actual force structures, capabilities and dispositions in Europe.

We believe that a secure peace can not be achieved without steady progress on all aspects of the confrontation which has divided Europe for more than four decades. Moreover, redressing the disparity in conventional forces in Europe would remove an obstacle to the achievement of the better political relationship between all states of Europe to which we aspire. Conventional arms control must therefore be seen as part of a dynamic process which addresses the military, political, and human aspects of this division.

You may discover other ways of using the Roman Room System and Mind Mapping together. With practice, you'll find that the two techniques can be used quite effectively, especially when you have to learn large amounts of information.

Word Substitution is one of those techniques that most people like immediately. It's fun to make up substitute words and phrases, especially silly ones. And the sillier the better!

You can apply Word Substitution to many memory situations. It's mostly a matter of applying the Basic Memory Principles of imagination and association.

Of course one of the more powerful applications of Word Substitution is in the task of matching up faces, names, and jobs. This is actually another instance where you can use more than one technique—in fact you must.

First you must be able quickly to pick out the dominant or unique feature in the face. Then you've got to create a substitute for the name. Then you need to create a mental image representing the person's job. Then you must be able to use linking to combine the substitute name and the occupation activity in some fantasy involving that dominant or unique facial feature.

You can extend the scope of the method to include any other information about the person. For example, you can memorize the name of the person's spouse or children, or hobbies. Just be sure that you have a particular way of knowing what category of information you're memorizing. For example, I suggested using *hands activity* to represent the occupation. You might associate the *heart* with family information.

Although we only worked with last names, you can easily apply Word Substitution to remembering first names too. Just work with both the first and last name when you make up a substitution for the name. For example, for **Ike Cohen** you can substitute "**icon**" (a figure or image). Try the following practice exercise, which includes first names.

EXERCISE 2:   Each of the following faces has a name (first and last) and occupation. Spending no more than 15 seconds per face, memorize the faces, full names, and occupations. Then recall all the information on the page that follows.

name: Hector Chavez
occupation: Doctor

name: George Brown
occupation: Handyman

name: Joyce Jameson
occupation: Travel agent

name: Sylvia McCarthy
occupation: Store manager

name: Dan Chung
occupation: Engineer

name: Jan Crosby
occupation: Ad executive

name: Stephanie Harris
occupation: Bank teller

name: Pierre Martine
occupation: College professor

name:
occupation:

name:
occupation:

name:
occupation:

name:
occupation:

name:

occupation:

name:

occupation:

name:

occupation:

name:

occupation:

BREAK POINT

EXERCISE 3: Thoroughly analyze your performance in these last two exercises. If you made recall errors try to figure out why. Determine what specific aspect of the exercise gave you the most trouble. Then go back to the appropriate section of this book and do some additional work. Make up some practice exercises of your own. Afterward, look for opportunities in your daily life to apply the techniques.

Remember, you can take more than the specified time to learn the techniques in this program, if you need to. The important thing is that you actually master these powerful techniques!

Finally, here are some additional tips for learning the names and so on of people you've just met:

- Try to relax. There's a natural tendency to be nervous when meeting someone new. Of course we want them to like us, and we hope that they are someone we in turn will like. Also, if you believe that you easily forget new names, that alone will cause you to forget.
- Help others to remember *your* name. Remember that most people have this problem. So help them—and help yourself relax—by repeating your own name, during conversation, for example. One technique I've used is to point to my reddish beard and say, "Eric, as in Eric the Red."
- Use the other person's name in conversation. The more you repeat it, the more easily you'll be able to associate it with that person.
- Get into the habit of introducing people you've just met to other people you know, at a party for instance. Don't worry if you make a mistake or forget someone's name. That person will surely be ready to say it as soon as you stumble. And everyone will admire you for correctly remembering even a few!
- If you don't hear a name clearly, ask the person to repeat it. If it's an unusual name ask for the spelling. Or even the derivation. Aside from helping your memory, the person will surely be impressed with your interest.
- If you have some time between conversations at a party you can look at the crowd and practice going over the names and occupations to yourself.
- When you leave, repeat the person's name once again. As you do so, look at the face carefully and quickly review in your mind whatever associations you've created.
- When you get home, close your eyes and recall all the information you committed to memory about each person you met. Do it again the next day, and once each day for as long as you need to.

DAY 10

TECHNIQUE: MENTAL REHEARSAL

There is a belief that has been gaining credibility among psychologists and cognitive scientists. It is that the human mind cannot tell the difference between an *imagined experience* and an *actual experience*. Consequently, if you rehearse an activity in your mind, it has the same effect *on your mind* as if you actually carried out the activity.

This is a basic assumption underlying many adult learning programs such as success motivation, behavioral change using hypnosis, learning with subliminal programming, and gold medal achievement among champion athletes.

In success motivation seminars, for example, participants are taught to imagine themselves actually achieving their goals. This is a way to rehearse success in their minds.

Under hypnosis, a subject's mind is given a new instruction to follow, such as "You have no desire to smoke."

Subliminal programming feeds new information, such as words in a foreign language, into the unconscious mind of the learner.

Champion athletes preview their performances, such as making a high dive, over and over again in their minds, prior to their actual performance.

Many people report success with such methods in these areas and others. But also important is what can be learned from these experiences and applied to memory improvement.

Suppose you had just recently learned to play golf, and now you're back in your city apartment wishing you could be out practicing your sand shots so that you don't forget your most recent lesson. Do you suppose you could gain something from closing your eyes and imagining yourself hitting perfect sand blasts, just as the instructor showed you? Could you imagine yourself lifting the club and striking precisely, and could you imagine the nice feel of proper contact and the perfect explosion of the ball out of the trap on its way toward the pin, just as you've seen your instructor demonstrate? Of course you could.

What you gain from mental rehearsal is the ingraining of the desired behavior or information. It's your attempt to create new habits in your mind. Even if you can't *physically* practice the new habits you can at least give your *mind* the experience of practicing them.

You can use Mental Rehearsal for several memory problems. Some of these are packing for a trip, locating lost items, getting chores done, and performing in public. We'll look at each of these applications in some detail in a moment. But first, here are some general guidelines for using Mental Rehearsal effectively.

1. Mental Rehearsal is not the same thing as obsessing or worrying. Those are emotional responses. Mental Rehearsal is a technique that you use in a deliberate, rational way. You can be emotional, but it's because you *choose* to behave that way, such as a parent mentally rehearsing how he will angrily reprimand his child for bad behavior. He might go over in his mind the words he plans to use and the mood he wants to convey. But this is deliberate planning. Obsession and worry, on the other hand, occur when you cannot stop yourself from thinking about what you've done or plan to do.

2. Use your imagination. To use Mental Rehearsal effectively you've got to give your mind as complete an experience as possible. In the golf example, for instance, let your mind hear the *swoosh* of the club and feel the sand grains on your face. Apply the Basic Memory Principles, such as involving all of your senses.

3. Focus on details. The human mind has a great appetite for details. It will remember the smallest details for long periods of time, so long as those details have been well implanted at the beginning. The world-class tennis pro, for example, can run through the anticipated match in vivid detail, mentally practicing in advance his specific reactions to various shots.

4. Try to relax. This will help you to have a full, rich mental rehearsal. It'll also help to prepare you to be relaxed when you need to actually do what you have to do. If you're preparing to go on a trip, for example, relaxation will help calm the natural anxiety most

people feel when they are about to travel. (I've used this with friends who have travel anxiety. I tell them to close their eyes and rehearse traveling in their mind—imagine themselves veteran travelers. We talk them through all of the travel routines, and when we are done they feel more relaxed.)

5. Have a positive attitude. By thinking positively, you prepare your mind to experience success. If you have to deliver a speech, imagine that you will do well, that you will feel good about yourself, that you will remember what you have to remember, and that the audience will like you. This puts you in a class with Olympic gold medal winners who can't afford to have a negative attitude slow them down.

6. The more you mentally rehearse something the better you will ingrain the experience. But this also means that you've got to be careful not to mentally rehearse the wrong thing. For example, if you are trying to mentally rehearse a dance step you've just learned, and you're rehearsing it incorrectly, you will only be learning the wrong thing extremely well!

7. Connect with how you feel as you mentally rehearse. If you're preparing a presentation, for example, notice your feelings as you go through it in your mind. Is there something about it that makes you feel uncomfortable? If so, perhaps you ought to take another look at the content or purpose of your presentation.

8. Try playing different roles. In the case of preparing a presentation, for example, you might try imagining that you're in the audience. How do you react as a listener? Are you hostile or receptive? Are you bored or excited? I often use this sort of Mental Rehearsal when preparing to give a seminar or talk.

APPLICATION: PACKING FOR A TRIP

When I first started traveling extensively on business I would write myself a packing checklist each time. Later I tried writing one standard checklist that I could use for every trip. But there were always differences: Different clothes were required for different climates, different numbers of items were required for different lengths of stay, different materials were needed for different seminars or talks, and so on.

I also discovered that writing a checklist created a potential problem. Because I was learning to depend on the list, I would tend to forget to take anything that was not on the list. But it always seemed silly to put everything—especially the obvious items—on the list. So I concluded that while a written list was a good way to remember to take most things, it was also a good way to forget to take others!

Eventually I decided not to waste my time bothering with a written list. It often seemed to be such a time waster anyway. I'd write the list well in advance, spend time making changes in it over the next few days, and then hardly even follow it when it came time to pack!

I now use a form of Mental Rehearsal when packing for a trip. Specifically, I create a mental checklist as I pack to be sure I've included everything I need. There are two basic ways to do this, and I've found both to be quite effective.

1. Use your body as a checklist.

When you're ready to pack, start at the top of your head and, moving down to your feet, use every part of your body to remind yourself what to take.

When at your **head** you might decide to take a hat. At your **neck** you remember to pack some ties. When you get to your **waist** you are reminded to pack a belt. At your **ankles** you are prompted to pack some socks. And so on.

I reserve my **hands** to remind me to take whatever materials I need for my actual work: seminar materials, speech, writing instruments.

For cosmetics such as shampoo, razor, and tooth brush, I have a separate toiletries bag ready to drop into the suitcase. It contains everything I would need for a five-day trip.

EXERCISE 1: Pretend you've got to go on a two-day business trip to deliver a talk, "Success Through Better Memory," at a corporate conference. Use your body as a mental checklist to decide what you've got to pack. Imagine yourself actually putting the items in your suitcase(s). Try to be thorough but don't spend more than five minutes on it.

2. Use your activities as a checklist.

This method is slightly different but still uses a mental checklist at the time you are actually ready to pack.

Think about each activity you'll have to perform, in sequence. For each activity decide what items you will need and pack them. The first activity might be getting there. For that you might need your plane tickets, driver's license, credit card. When you get to your hotel you will go to sleep, and for that you'll need to pack pajamas. In the morning you'll meet your client for breakfast, and that reminds you to pack your gray suit, red tie, and pink shirt. And so on.

EXERCISE 2: Follow the instructions for the previous exercise, but this time use the "activities checklist" instead of the "body checklist."

EXERCISE 3: Spend a few moments comparing the two methods you've just practiced. Did you feel more comfortable with one than the other? Did you feel one was more effective than the other?

You can actually use both of these methods, one following the other. I often do that, particularly when I have several different activities to perform on a single trip, such as deliver a speech in one place or time, then a seminar in another, then meet with a client to plan a future program. First I use the body checklist and then, to be sure I've packed everything I'll need, I use the activities checklist.

Whichever way you do it, you'll find that using a mental checklist to pack for a trip will help remove much of the hassle of traveling. I've found it to be more effective than a written checklist, since it's always available yet flexible.

Just be sure to apply the general guidelines mentioned earlier, especially the use of imagination, relaxation, and focus on detail. If you do, you'll find this technique to be yet another opportunity to stretch those memory muscles!

BREAK POINT

APPLICATION: GETTING CHORES DONE

You can use Mental Rehearsal to help you get chores done. This is similar to using an activities checklist in packing for a trip. The idea is simple: Mentally rehearse the chores you have to do, before you do them. The result will be that you'll remember to do them, and you'll do them effectively.

Here is an example. Suppose you have to do the following chores one day:

1. Leave the house at 9:30 A.M.
2. Stop at the bank to pick up some cash.
3. Arrive at your hairdresser for your 10:30 appointment. Leave by 11:30.
4. Go to the supermarket; shop and ask that it be delivered to your home at 5:00.
5. Go to the gym for your regular 1:00 aerobics class. Leave by 1:45.
6. Meet your friend for lunch uptown at 2:15. Leave by 3:30.
7. Pick up your daughter at school at 4:00.
8. Stop at the bakery on the way home. Buy a loaf of rye.
9. Arrive at home by 5:00.

You can mentally rehearse all of these activities just before you leave the house, and it need only take a minute or two. Imagine yourself looking at the clock, seeing 9:30 (actually visualize the big hand and the little hand, or the digits if it's a digital), and picture yourself leaving the house, closing and locking the door. Visualize yourself walking left, down the street to the bank, going in and using the cash machine. See yourself turning right as you leave the bank, to head for the bus stop where you can get the crosstown bus to take you to your hairdresser. See a clear picture of yourself arriving as your watch shows 10:30. Imagine your hairdresser working on you, and then leaving when the clock on the wall near the exit says 11:30. Picture yourself taking the bus back across town, walking up to the supermarket, shopping and asking for the delivery at 5:00 (you know that's when you'll arrive home), and so forth.

If you mentally rehearse all of these activities in advance, your mind will know what to do at the proper moment and you won't have to worry about forgetting an appointment or being late. It will almost be as though you've already done these things, and now you are just doing them again. (Of course you *have* already done all of these things, at least in your *mind*.)

The more clearly you can visualize your actual movements, feelings, and thoughts in advance, the more easily and effectively you'll be able to carry out the chores. And don't forget to follow the general guidelines for Mental Rehearsal discussed earlier.

If you've only got enough time to use this technique once, it's best to use it just before your activities (just before you leave the house). If you have more time, however, you can rehearse over and over again beginning a day or more in advance. But remember that the more time between rehearsal and actual behavior the more chance for forgetting, and so the more need for practice.

EXERCISE 3:   First, write down ten activities you've got to do tomorrow, starting and ending at some specific times. Then, sitting in a relaxed position, mentally rehearse those activities.

EXERCISE 4:   Repeat the previous exercise, but for *everything* you must do the day after tomorrow. In other words, mentally rehearse the entire day, from beginning to end. Be sure to include lots of details, including your probable thoughts and feelings, and the possible reactions of others.

APPLICATION: PERFORMING IN PUBLIC

Performing in public can include delivering a speech to an audience of five hundred, giving a sales presentation to a new client, asking your boss for a raise, scolding your child, or playing a part in a school play. It can even include nonverbal activities, such as putting on a juggling act, dancing at a discotheque, or running a pass pattern in a football game.

You can mentally rehearse these kinds of performances in advance in a similar way as you rehearse your daily chores. By rehearsing mentally you'll be training your mind, even if you cannot train your body.

Suppose, for example, that your brother asks you to be best man at his upcoming wedding. It'll be a big wedding and your brother is counting on the rather elaborate ceremony to go smoothly. You, unfortunately, cannot attend the rehearsal. So you ask your brother to send you a script of the ceremony and give him your assurance that you'll be prepared.

If you're skilled at Mental Rehearsal you ought to be able to read through the script *on your way to the wedding*, memorize your part, and perform your role correctly. I know it's possible to do this sort of thing, for I've done similar things on many occasions!

EXERCISE 5: Write down three "performances" you must give in the next few months. Mentally rehearse each one in vivid detail, making sure to apply the general guidelines for Mental Rehearsal. In each case, try to answer the following questions during your rehearsal:

1. What must you do, step by step?
2. What must you say (either word for word or just the ideas)?
3. What mood do you want to create?
4. What are the audience's expectations?
5. How do you feel while doing this?
6. How does the audience react during and after your performance?
7. How do you feel after your performance?

BREAK POINT

APPLICATION: LOCATING LOST ITEMS

You can also use Mental Rehearsal to locate lost items, a common complaint of those who consider themselves "forgetful."

Instead of rehearsing in advance, however, you need to mentally "play back" your recent activity. It's like an instant replay. Just use the technique of Mental Rehearsal to visualize yourself retracing your steps.

Suppose, for example, you arrive home and realize that you don't have the umbrella that you know you left the house with three hours before. Start by going back in your mind to the last time you remember having it. Be sure it's a strong vivid image. Suppose you only remember leaving the house with it. Okay, then follow your activity in your mind, down the elevator, to the post office. What did you do there? Did you put the umbrella down on the counter? When you left, what did you have in your hands? (How did you open the door to leave?) Where did you go next? And so on.

If you've developed the skill of Mental Rehearsal you ought to be able to apply it to this common memory problem.

EXERCISE 6: Select an object, such as your umbrella, briefcase, gloves, hat, eyeglasses, or purse, that you carried with you recently (yesterday or the day before). Use Mental Rehearsal to follow that item through your day, from beginning to end. Be sure you can see the item in every activity.

If you have difficulty, stop and examine that activity carefully until you can see the item there.

TECHNIQUE: RHYMES AND SAYINGS

APPLICATION: MEMORIZING BITS OF FACT AND TRIVIA

For most of us it's been many years since grade school. However, I'll bet most remember the saying "I before E, except after C." Despite the passage of time, people remember it because it's cute, cool, neat, nifty, or whatever your generation would call it. But it's certainly timeless, for I know it's still taught to youngsters today.

This is a typical example of a saying that can help us remember a rule of grammar. We remember the rule because we remember the saying, and we remember the saying because it's more fun to remember a saying than to remember a rule of grammar.

The same holds for rhymes. In fact, the above saying is really part of a rhyme:

> I before E,
> Except after C,
> And when pronounced A,
> As in "neighbor" and "weigh."*

Such rhymes and sayings can be useful memory aids, particularly for miscellaneous bits of fact and trivia such as dates, rules of grammar, rules of arithmetic, or rules of thumb. Here are some common examples:

- Setting Daylight Saving Time and Standard Time
     Spring forward,
     Fall backward.
- How many days in each month
     Thirty days has September,
     April, June, and November.
     All the rest have thirty-one,
     Except the second month, we find,
     Has twenty-eight, till leap year gives it twenty-nine

---

*There are exceptions, of course, such as "either," "foreign," "height," "seize," and "weird."

- When Columbus discovered America
  In fourteen hundred and ninety-two,
  Columbus sailed the ocean blue.
- When the Spanish Armada was defeated
  The Spanish Armada met its fate
  In fifteen hundred and eighty-eight.
- When the Fire of London occurred
  In Sixteen hundred and sixty-six,
  London burned like rotten sticks.
- When the American Civil War began
  When the North the South did shun,
  T'was eighteen hundred sixty-one.
- When the American Civil War ended
  When the Union did survive,
  T'was eighteen hundred sixty-five.
- How to treat illness
  Feed a cold.
  Starve a fever.
- How to solve a proportion.
  The product of the means
  Equals the product of the extremes.
- How to remember five streets in San Francisco (Post, Sutter, Bush, Pine, and California)
  The postman at Sutter's Mill
  Was bushed from pining for California.

EXERCISE 7: Write down some rhymes or sayings you've come across that are used to aid memory. Here are some categories that might help trigger your memory:

Dates of important events	Science and weather
Names of places	Geography
Rules of grammar	Food and drink
Rules of arithmetic or mathematics	Medicine
Rules in a foreign language	Sports and entertainment
Religion	Folklore

DAY 11

TECHNIQUE: PHYSICAL PATTERNS

Patterns are a great memory aid. Just think of how easy it would be to spell if all words were spelled exactly as they sound. Unfortunately, it just isn't that way in English. Consider words like "height," in which only the first, third and last letter are sounded. Or "queue" in which only the first letter is pronounced.

In many situations patterns already exist. Recognizing these patterns can be a great aid to memory. In cases where they do not exist, however, we can create them. This can make it easier to remember all sorts of things.

One of the types of patterns we can use is physical patterns. For example, there is the old advice that if you want to remember something you should tie a string around your finger. The thinking behind that advice is that when you later see the string tied around your finger you will say to yourself one of two things:

If you *always* tie a string around your finger when you want to remember something, seeing the string will prompt you to say: "There's that string. There is something I must remember, for that is what the string always means."

If you *never* tie a string around your finger, seeing that string will prompt you to say: "Why is there a string around my finger? It must mean something special. Let me try to remember."

In either case, the string around your finger represents a physical pattern that is designed to trigger recall, for it forces you to search for its meaning. Once you've done that, you're well on your way to remembering what you've got to remember. (At least you now know there's something to remember!)

I use this technique often in my office. Suppose, for example, I'm boiling water for coffee in the kitchen. To remind myself of that I switch my wristwatch from my left to my right hand. This is actually a *disruption* of a physical pattern, for I normally wear my watch on my left hand. But it has the same effect, for when I see it I realize that the different pattern has a meaning, and this forces me to think of the meaning. Once I focus on its meaning there's a good chance I'll remember its significance, thereby saving another pot from meltdown!

APPLICATION: FINDING YOUR WAY

You can use physical patterns to remember directions. Consider, for example, the common problem of parking your car in a big lot and having to remember where you parked it. Here's how you can use physical patterning:

> First, pick some fixed point near where you are going, such as a particular store entrance. Then, as you walk from your car to that fixed point draw a picture in your mind of your path and count your steps. Perhaps you first walk straight for 60 steps and then turn left for 30 steps. If you were to visualize that as a line drawing, you would see that it can be represented by the letter L in which the vertical line is twice as long as the horizontal line. Now you just have to remember the physical image of such an L in order to retrace your steps to your car.
>
> Sometimes there are other physical points that you can use as well. In large parking lots, for example, you can count rows and columns of cars, instead of your own steps. Or you can count light posts.

Of course that was a simple example. But you can use this technique for complicated directions, too. Instead of trying to remember turns, sign posts and street names, you might just draw a mental picture in your mind. For example, "straight, left, and right" puts you on a "backward Z" headed in the same direction as you started, just farther to the left. This works particularly well when you've got to go in a general direction rather than to a specific spot, such as back to a main highway.

It also helps if you have a good understanding of north, east, west, and south. And knowing that the sun rises in the east and sets in the west is mandatory!

Here's another illustration of how you can use physical patterns to find your way. Many cities are organized in a particular way. In Manhattan, for example, First, Third, and Madison Avenues on the East Side run uptown only (north), while Second, Lexington, and Fifth avenues run downtown (south). Most of the cross streets are numbered and increase as you go uptown. Also, for the most part, even-numbered streets run from west to east and odd-numbered streets east to west. Understanding these physical patterns makes remembering how to get from place to place easy in a place like Manhattan!

EXERCISE 1:   Name some natural physical patterns in your city or town that would make it easy for a visitor to remember directions. If you live in Italy, for example, you could tell people that you live in the country that's shaped like a boot on the world map.

EXERCISE 2:   Think of some way in which you use physical patterns to aid your memory of directions. Pretend you have to explain it to someone else. How does it work?

EXERCISE 3:   Think of a new physical pattern that you could use from now on to aid your memory.

TECHNIQUE: WORD PATTERNS

APPLICATION: MEMORIZING BITS OF FACT AND TRIVIA

Word patterns are great aids for memory, and they are fun to create. The idea is simply to find some way of creating a pattern among the words so that you'll more easily remember them.
    As an example, consider the saying used earlier:

> Feed a cold.
> Starve a fever.

The saying helps to remind us of the general rule of thumb. But people often confuse it as follows:

> Starve a cold.
> Feed a fever.

To solve this memory problem, just look for some pattern you can make out of the words in the correct version of the saying. For example, notice that the letters of the key words are in alphabetical order going down (vertically). That is, "F" in "Feed" comes before "S" in "Starve" and "c" in "cold" comes before "f" in "fever." Or you can use this pattern: In the last line ("Starve a fever") both words have the letter "v."

To illustrate another principle of word patterning, consider how children are taught to memorize the spelling of Mississippi. They are taught to *regroup* the word, and think of it as composed of several subgroups: M i ss i ss i pp i (say "double s" and "double i"). You can always look for opportunities to regroup words and phrases to make them easier to remember.

Another word pattern technique is to use *acronyms*. For example, common advice to runners with sore legs is to use R.I.C.E., which stands for "Rest, Ice, Compression and Elevation." There are many common acronyms around. But you can always create your own!

Below are some additional examples of the use of word patterns.

Word/Expression	Word Pattern/Memory Aid
Roger Redding (a name)	Both first and last names begin with "R," as in Rail Road.
Gary Yodoff (a name)	Last name ends in "y" and first name begins in "Y."
Francis or Frances?	Francis has an "i" (so does "him"). Frances has an "e" (so does "her").
Stationary or stationery?	"Stationery" has the word "one" embedded in it. Think of "one sheet." Then you will also know the other must be "stationary."
Principal or principle?	Remember that the principal is your *pal*. Then you'll also remember the other word.
How to spell "easel."	Notice the letters "sel." You can use an easel to *sell* (give a sales presentation).
Port or starboard?	Port is "left," and both have four letters. So starboard is "right."
Stalactite or stalagmite?	The first has a "c" as in "ceiling." The second has a "g" as in "ground."
The Great Lakes: Huron, Ontario, Michigan, Erie, and Superior	H.O.M.E.S.

EGBDF, the names of the lines of the treble staff	Every Good Boy Does Fine.
Sine: *Opposite over Hypotenuse* Cosine: *Adjacent over Hypotenuse* Tangent: *Opposite over Adjacent*	Indian Chief SOH-CAH-TOA
Three major avenues in NYC *Ma*dison, *P*ark, *Lex*ington.	Maple

EXERCISE 4:   In your notebook, add at least six well-known items to the above list. On the left side write down the words or expressions that cause the memory problem. Include names of people and places, spelling problems, or word confusion. On the right write down the word pattern that you use as a memory aid.

EXERCISE 5:   Repeat the previous exercise, except do not use any well-known word pattern items. Instead, make up six of your own.

BREAK POINT

TECHNIQUE: NUMBER PATTERNS

APPLICATION: REMEMBERING NUMBERS, PRICES, AND TELEPHONE NUMBERS

Just as you can use word patterns to remember verbal or written material, you can use number patterns to remember all sorts of numbers. And in the number-oriented world of today, that's important.

   Of course you can usually resort to writing down the numbers you need to remember, especially important numbers like your Social Security number. But there are times when that's not possible or practical. Here are a few examples:

Identification Numbers

How often have you been asked for your license plate number and had to go out in the rain to look at it on the car? Wouldn't it be nice if you knew it? It would also make finding your car in a big lot easier, if you happen to own a popular model.

Combination locks can be a problem. Where do you write down the number? When I was in school I used to scratch the number onto the back of the lock itself, in a special code of course. But after a while it wears down.

If you're in business you might have to know model numbers or stock numbers. Or if you're just out shopping for an item and want to compare prices in different stores, you need to remember the model number. In both cases, the hectic atmosphere of a retail store might make it difficult to rely on pencil and paper.

Prices

Comparison shopping requires that you remember prices, too. Suppose you just happen to be in a store one day and see an item you've been looking for. But you don't have your list with you, so you can't decide whether it's selling at a better price. Wouldn't it be nice if you remembered the other prices?

If you run a retail store people naturally expect you to know prices of the merchandise. They also tend to become distrustful if you've always got to look up a price. And executives who don't know the prices of the items their company sells appear to be out of touch with the customer.

Telephone Numbers

Suppose you're in a phone booth and have to call information for a number and don't have any way to write it down. You've just got to memorize the number until you can dial it.

If you have a cellular phone in your car it's not a good idea to have to look up every number while driving. If you don't have a phone with memory, you'll have to rely on your own.

Emergency numbers are best memorized. You don't want to have to scurry around to look up the number of the local fire department while your garage is going up in a blaze!

Other Numbers

Suppose you're counting out cards, or sheets of paper, or whatever, and the telephone rings. You answer the phone and have a conversation. Ten minutes later, when you hang up, you go back to your task. But you've forgotten what number you were up to and so you've got to start all over again!

In a similar situation, you might be reading a book and need to put it down. Of course you can use a bookmark, or dog-ear the page, or place the book upside down. But you know, I'm sure, the disadvantages of those methods: There may be no bookmark nearby, dog-earring damages the page, and upside-down books always seem to manage to right themselves! Wouldn't it be nice if you could just make a quick mental note of the page you're up to?

There are many techniques you can use to memorize numbers. They're all easy to apply and can even be fun. Although we'll look at each one individually, you'll quickly see that they can be combined. That is, for any particular situation you might apply more than one technique.

The basic idea is similar to that underlying word patterns: Look for a pattern, or create a pattern, that will turn something unfamiliar into something familiar, something forgettable into something memorable.

Grouping and Regrouping

The average adult can hold seven digits in short-term memory. For strings of digits longer than seven, the tendency is to forget the digits near the middle. For these reasons, grouping can be an effective memory technique for numbers.

Suppose, for example, you tried to memorize the nine-digit number 101368733 in the usual way. You would find it easy to remember the first few (101) and the last few (733) but would have a hard time recalling the middle ones (368). So, try instead to memorize the number grouped this way: 101-36-8733. Now it's easier to remember. (Notice that the new pattern is like a Social Security number.)

You can also regroup numbers that have already been grouped. For example, suppose you wanted to memorize the telephone number 545-4733. If you regroup the digits you get a number pattern that's much easier to remember: 5454-733. (I know, it looks funny. But it comes out the same when you dial it!)

It also helps to say the number out loud, emphasizing the grouping you've chosen to use. This is particularly true with telephone numbers. In fact, the simple act of repeating, out loud, a number the operator has just given you will usually implant the number in your short-term memory long enough for you to dial it correctly.

Simple Mental Arithmetic

Now don't get nervous, it says *simple*. For example, suppose you had to memorize the phone number 716-3264. Set aside the first digit, 7, for the moment, and just look at the digits 163264. Think of them regrouped this way: 16-32-64. Now here's the simple arithmetic: 16 doubled equals 32, and then doubled again equals 64. Tack on the 7 at the beginning and you've got the number memorized.

Now you might be thinking "That's still complicated." Not really. It just sounds complicated because it has to be explained in words, on paper. But to your mind it's a very simple number pattern that you can easily learn with little effort. Just don't be afraid of the numbers!

EXERCISE 6: Use grouping and/or arithmetic to memorize the following numbers. Reminder: You can often use "powers." For example, "3 raised to the second power" means "3 times 3" which equals 9. Similarly, "2 raised to the third power" means "2 times 2 times 2" which equals 8.

1. 799-3618
2. 423-5279
3. 8642117908
4. 884-49-9760
5. 213-476-1882
6. 965432379986

Numbers of Special Significance

There are many special numbers with which you are already very familiar. For example, you know that there are 24 hours in a day and 36 inches in a yard, and that 986 are the digits of normal body temperature (98.6 ° Fahrenheit.) You also know the date (one or two digits), month (one or two digits), and year (two or four digits) of your birth. You might remember the prices of items you buy frequently—just drop the dollar sign and decimal point. If you're a sports fan you also must know the jersey numbers of your favorite players.

All of these are examples of established number associations already well implanted in your mind. You can use these, together with linking, to memorize new numbers.

A well-known example of this kind of linking is the height of Mount Fujiyama in Japan, which is 12,365 feet. Notice the patterns: 12 months in a year and 365 days in a year. You can use linking to associate Mount Fujiyama with the image of a year—months and days.

Suppose I had to memorize the 10-digit number 1946561995. First I would group it as follows: 1946-56-1995. Now, the first group, 1946, is the year of my birth. The second group, 56, is the number of Lawrence Taylor, New York Giants linebacker and one of my heroes. The last group, 1995, is the price ($19.95) of my first book. Now all I need to do is create some silly mental fantasy to link these three groups, such as "I was **born** (in another life) as **Lawrence Taylor**, became famous and published a **book** on Creative Thinking Skills that was a big seller."

You're probably thinking how convenient that these three groups were numbers I already knew. Of course it's a made-up example. But there are so many familiar number patterns that have significance to you personally, or in general, that it should be easy to find them everywhere. You've just got to be willing to see them!

Here's another example. Suppose you were reading a book and had to put it down to answer the telephone. If you were up to page 52 you could say to yourself, "I've done a year's worth of reading." The conclusion is so absurd that you couldn't help but remember it for the few moments you need to. And don't worry about later confusing it with 12 (as in 12 weeks) or 365 (as in 365 days) because you will know that those numbers couldn't be right.

You can also create significance where there is none. For example, if you were trying to memorize Fred's phone number, say 887-4252, you could memorize the last part with a made-up fantasy like "I know he's 42 years old, but he looks 10 years older—52."

A special tip for telephone numbers: You can often convert the numbers to letters that have significance. Just look on your telephone key pad for the corresponding letters. For example, when a friend of mine moved I discovered that his new phone number translated to TY1-CLIP. That was much easier to remember than the actual number.

Another special tip for telephone numbers: Each digit also has special significance because of its *position* on the key pad. You might be able to memorize a telephone number by the geometric pattern it traces as you move from key to key. For example, it might form a square with a line across the center.

EXERCISE 7: Look at the following list of some standard numbers of significance. Add any that occur to you that are not on the list. Think of at least 20 special numbers of your own (i.e., numbers that have personal significance to you) and write them in your notebook.

Number	Significance
12	Months in a year; a dozen; half a day (12 hours)
13	Baker's dozen; unlucky number
24	24 hours in a day; two dozen
25	A quarter (25 cents)
26	Half a year (26 weeks); half a deck of cards
28	The number of teams in the National Football League
36	36 inches in a yard
49	California Gold Rush, 1849
52	Weeks in a year; cards in a deck
59	Bloomingdale's stop on the IRT train in Manhattan (59th St.)
60	Seconds in a minute; minutes in an hour
76	Year of U.S. Independence, 1776
365	Days in a year
986	Normal body temperature, 98.6° Fahrenheit
1492	Columbus discovered America
29975	Price of your new car ($29,975)
362417	Your combination lock number

EXERCISE 8: Memorize the following numbers using the method of numbers of significance.

1. 361-2365
2. 544-0986
3. 9875481267
4. 099-66-4570
5. 315-986-1215
6. 921630839873
7. 27209886477436
8. 82446723920573

Number Rhyme and Link

Using your number rhyme pegs, together with linking, is an ideal way to give meaning to numbers. Here's how it works: Suppose you want to memorize the number 2873. If your number rhyme pegs are the same as mine, you would have: "shoe, gate, heaven, tree" for "two, eight, seven, three." Now link these four words into something like: "An enormous **shoe** kicks a huge white **gate** all the way up to **heaven**, where it is caught by the outstretched branches of a big spreading **tree**." Or else create separate fantasies to link each pair in the usual way.

Later, remembering the silly fantasy or fantasies will trigger your number rhyme pegs, which in turn you will quickly convert to the digits of the number. It's really that simple! It makes use of what you already know.

EXERCISE 9: Memorize the following numbers using the Number Rhyme and Link systems.

1. 94867
2. 325-8754
3. 374564466
4. 865-12-4543
5. 921630839873
6. 25498916387686

Some final bits of advice on using number patterns. Aside from the methods I've demonstrated here there are ones you might make up for yourself. As always, the techniques you make up yourself will always work best for you, so be open to the possibilities.

Ultimately you want to use whichever technique works best for the situation. Sometimes that means having to choose between two or more approaches. Don't get stuck over the decision. It isn't so important. In fact, in most cases you'll probably use a combination of several techniques.

You may find it best to try certain approaches first, depending upon the *length* of the number. Here's what I've found, but feel free to adapt it to your own liking:

Size of Number	Pattern to Look for
1 digit	Age of a child; number of a baseball or football jersey; a lucky number
2 digits	Age of an adult; number on a baseball or football jersey; money (25 cents); unit of measure (12 inches); years ('76)
3 digits	Arithmetic (3 + 2 = 5); prices ($1.95)
4 digits	Years; prices; arithmetic (6 x 7 = 42)
5 digits	Group 3-2 or 2-3
6 digits	Group 3-3 or 4-2 or 2-4
7 digits	Group 3-4 (as a telephone number) or 4-3
9 digits	Group 3-2-4 (as a S.S. number) or 3-3-3
14 digits	Group as two telephone numbers

DAY 12

TECHNIQUE: THE NUMERICAL CODE SYSTEM

The Numerical Code System is probably the most comprehensive of all the techniques we'll study. It's also the most powerful. You can use this technique to memorize practically anything. But we'll focus on how to use it to memorize numbers, prices, and dates, for those are the areas in which the technique has its greatest value.

This technique is another of the peg systems. It's been around for over 300 years and is based on a fixed set of pegs for the digits 0 through 9. The pegs are particular letters of the alphabet.

Here's how the technique works: Since every number is composed of some combination of the same ten digits, 0 through 9, you can translate any length number into a sequence of these special pegs. And since the pegs are letters, once you've strung them together you can create words, and even phrases, from them. You then memorize the words or phrases using our other systems, especially linking.

The first step is to learn the memory pegs. Read through them, below, but be sure to also read the explanation that follows.

Digit	Numerical Code Peg
0	s, z, soft c
1	d, t, th
2	n
3	m
4	r
5	l
6	j, sh, ch, dg, soft g
7	k, ch, hard c, hard g, q
8	f, v, ph
9	p, b

The vowels ("a," "e," "i," "o" and "u") have no value, nor do the letters "w," "h" and "y." They are all disregarded. Silent letters are also disregarded. For example, in the word "lamb" the final "b" is silent, and therefore is disregarded. Double letters that produce the same sound count only once, such as the double "t" in "letter." The letter "x" is translated according to how it sounds in the word. It might sound like "ks" as in "axiom" or "ksh" as in "flexion," etc. In general, the way a letter is *sounded* in a particular word will always take predecence over the spelling of the word.

Now to explain the logic behind this selection of pegs. This should help you to memorize them.

Digit	Explanation of Code Peg
0	The first sound in the word "zero" has the same sound as these letters.
1	The letters "t" and "d" have one downstroke, and "th" has a similar sound as these letters.
2	The letter "n" has two downstrokes.
3	The letter "m" has three downstrokes.
4	The letter 'r' is the last letter in the word "four."
5	The capital letter "L" is the Roman numeral for 50. Or think of the shape of an L that your hand (5 fingers) can make when you hold it up.
6	The letter "j" is the mirror image of the digit 6; the other letter combinations all have basically the same sound.
7	The capital letter "K" almost looks as though it's composed of two 7's, one upside down and tilted slightly; the other letter combinations all have the same basic sound.
8	The letter "f" in script looks something like an 8; "ph" and "v" have the same sound.
9	The letter "p" is the mirror image of the digit 9; the letter "b" is an inverted "p" and also has a similar sound.

By now you've noticed that this system is dependent on the *sound* of letters, or combinations of letters. If you compare "j" and "sh," for example, you'll notice that your tongue, lips, and throat do the same things to produce both sounds.

To make it all crystal clear, let's look at some examples. In each case, we'll "translate" a word back to its numerical equivalent.

Consider the word "apple." Sound it out. Aside from the vowel, which doesn't count, all you hear is the sound of a "p" and the sound of an "l." So the numerical equivalent is 95.

In the word "lamb," all that count are the "l" and the "m" since the "b" is silent. So the word translates to 53.

In the word "flexible" the first sound is created by the letter "f," which is 8, then "l," or 5. Now we come to the letter "x." Say it slowly, out loud, and you will hear the sound of a "k" and "s" together. So the "x" will count as 7 and 0. The next consonant sound is produced by the letter "b," represented by 9, and finally another "l," for another 5. Stringing it all together we have the 6-digit number 857095.

Consider the word "position." The "p" is clearly 9, and the "s" a 0. But the "t" does not translate to a 1 as it normally would. Instead, it translates to a 6 because it sounds like "sh." The final sound, "n," is a 2, and so the word "position" translates to the number 9062.

EXERCISE 1: Translate each of the following words or phrases to its numerical equivalent. The correct answers follow on the next page. NOTE: Translate the phrases to single numerical strings.

Words/Phrases to Translate

1. mountain
2. elevator
3. puppeteers
4. paintings
5. emptiness
6. Maryland
7. children
8. Bienstock
9. gigantic
10. picturesque
11. interference
12. bacon and eggs
13. exasperating
14. photograph everything
15. ice melts in the summertime

Correct Numerical Translations

1. 3212
2. 5814
3. 99140
4. 92170
5. 39120
6. 34521
7. 65142
8. 92017
9. 67217
10. 976407
11. 2148420
12. 9722170
13. 70094127
14. 8174884127
15. 035102103413

EXERCISE 2: Study the numerical code pegs until you understand them thoroughly. Memorize them. Write out some words or phrases at random (use the dictionary to help pick them); translate them to digits.

Do this until you're very comfortable with the codes.

BREAK POINT

APPLICATION: REMEMBERING NUMBERS, PRICES, AND TELEPHONE NUMBERS

You can probably already see how powerful this system is, just from doing the previous exercises. And you may already be thinking of how you can use it.

One of the obvious ways to apply this technique is in the memorization of numbers: code numbers, ID numbers, model numbers, price numbers, telephone numbers, and so on. Here are the steps required:

1. Translate the number to letters, using the numerical code pegs.
2. Make up meaningful words or phrases from those letters by inserting vowels and silent letters wherever necessary. Use the Basic Memory Principles to make the words memorable.
3. Connect the words or phrases to the situation by using the Link System. You can also use Word Substitution, especially for names.

This method works for the simple reason that words, and fantasies based on those words, are far more memorable than numbers. Numbers are neutral; they have little glamour. Words and mental images, on the other hand, have much more interest, and are therefore easier to remember.

Here's an example. Suppose for some reason you had to remember the 11-digit number 94102842792. Translating this number using our numerical pegs yields the following letters as one possibility: brdsnfrngpn. Of course you could have selected the "p" for the 9 instead of the "b," or the "th" for the 1 instead of the "d." The important thing is to do it quickly; go with whatever comes to mind first. Now let's make sense of these eleven letters. Here are two different ways to go about it:

1. Inserting vowels, I come up with **birds in a frying pan.** Now that should be an easy mental image to remember. Far easier than the original 11-digit number!
2. Again inserting vowels I get these words: **bread sun frown go pen.** These five words can now be linked, perhaps like this:

bread → sun	**Bread** made to look like the **sun** (round and yellow).
sun → frown	The **sun** causes people to **frown** (instead of smile).
frown → go	A traffic cop who signals the cars to **go** simply by making a **frown.**
go → pen	Creating a huge GO sign (not a STOP sign) with a huge **pen.**

Either way you do it, you've replaced the job of memorizing an 11-digit number with the task of remembering some mental fantasy or fantasies. To recall the original number, just translate the key words back to digits using the code pegs.

(Incidentally, don't think that just because the first method takes fewer words to explain than the second, it's necessarily better. Remember that explaining on paper is quite different from how it actually works in the mind.)

For another example, suppose you had to remember that the price of a share of IBM stock was $135. Translating 135 yields the letters "tml." Now, that makes me think of the Mexican **tamale.** Link that word to an object that makes "IBM" more concrete, such as a **personal computer,** and you have the fantasy of **your PC covered in hot tamales!** Now you not only will remember the price, $135, but you've got it linked to IBM, through the image of the PC.

Notice that it wouldn't matter if you misspelled the word "tamales" and used "tomales" instead. The Numerical Code System cares only about *sound.*

You might wonder if you can get confused with such an image and think instead that the "PC" is the part that should be translated to a number, especially if you've got many such fantasies in your head at one time. But in actual practice it isn't a problem, for several reasons. One is that you need the fantasy for a relatively short period of time. Another is that since you were the one who created the fantasy, the mere act of creating it forced your mind to focus on the information; your mind will recognize its own work when it needs to. But also, the context of the situation will usually lead you to the right choice.

Suppose, in this last example, you're a stockbroker who deals with several computer companies. In that case you need to have a special image for each computer company. So for IBM the image of a PC will not work. Instead, for IBM you might use a **blue PC with pinstripes,** and for Unisys you might use a **mainframe cyclops** (a large computer with a single eye in the center!), and so on. You would probably want to use these images on a regular basis. And if you do, you'll never be confused as to which part of the fantasy represents the number.

For fractions you can decide to use some standard images. For example, you might use a **25-cent piece** to represent ¼; **half a grapefruit** to represent ½; a **three-quarter length coat** to represent ¾.

For eighths and sixteenths you might use a different method. For example, ⅜ can be thought of as simply 38 and ¹⁵/₁₆ can be thought of as

1516. Now there's no problem confusing any of these fractions with other fractions, since a stockbroker would only deal in these kinds of fractions. But you have to have a special way of knowing that a number, such as 1516, represents the fraction $^{15}/_{16}$ and not the number 1516. You might do this by visualizing all fractional images **inside a thimble.** Then, whenever your mental image includes something inside a thimble you automatically know that the translated number is a fraction.

In the case of the stockbroker, however, he'll probably know that a number such as 1516 cannot be the share price, although he might not be sure about a number like 38. In other words, the context of the particular situation often makes the true meaning of the number clear.

This last comment leads to another point. You should always try to know the format of the numbers you're dealing with, for that will always help. For example, Social Security numbers all have nine digits and telephone numbers have seven, or ten with area code. In your office, individual extensions might have one, two, three, or four digits. In your business, prices might all have three digits. If you have to deal in cents as well as dollars, you can either rely on your knowledge of the numbers or differentiate the cents from the dollars by using a special image such as the **thimble** for fractions.

Let's look at another example. Suppose you want to memorize the phone number of your dentist: 868-4902. Translating with the Numerical Code System you might get something like **fish for bison** (verify this before continuing!). Notice that you don't have to stick to the original grouping of the number. Now link this silly phrase to your dentist with something like: "I have to go to the **dentist** so he can **fish for bison** in my mouth, removing all those foul smelling creatures!"

With phone numbers, you can choose to use the person's occupation, such as dentist, or name, such as Dr. Jones. You can also use Word Substitution to help you. For example, you might use **Jonah** as a substitute for Dr. Jones, and then the fantasy would be "**Jonah** needs to feed the hungry whale, so he has to **fish for bison** in my mouth." (By the way, notice the sense of urgency in that image—that ought to get you to call for an appointment!)

If you need an area code, just tack it on; all it does is lengthen the phone number by three digits. But if you use certain area codes often and need to know what they are, you might want to prepare some standard translations that you'll always use. Then you won't have to make them up each time, and at the same time you can link the area code to the location. Below are some examples.

EXERCISE 3:   Study the following examples until you understand how they work. Then make up six of your own for area codes you often use.

Location	Area Code	Translation	Link Fantasy
NYC	212	Indian	**NYC** sold by an **Indian**
Los Angeles	213	Not me	Live in **LA? Not me!**
Miami	305	Mazel	What **mazel** ("luck" in Hebrew) to retire in **Miami**
Wyoming	307	Mask	**Yellow** bandit wears a **mask** (Yellowstone Nat'l Park)
Chicago	312	Mow down	The **wind** will **mow** you **down** ("Windy City")
Westchester	914	Butter	**Westchester** (wealthy suburb of NYC) people use real **butter**

EXERCISE 4:   In your notebook, write down the names and phone numbers of six people whose telephone numbers you don't already have memorized (e.g., your dentist, lawyer, golf partner). Then apply the technique (as used in the dentist example above) to create a mental image that is linked to that person. When you are done, study your mental images until you know them well. Practice recalling these over the next several days to store them permanently in your long-term memory.

Person	Phone #	Translation Word	Mental Image
1.			
2.			
3.			
4.			
5.			
6.			

BREAK POINT

APPLICATION: REMEMBERING APPOINTMENTS, SCHEDULES, AND DATES

In preparation for applying the Numerical Code System to times and dates, we need to cover another important aspect of this technique.

It may have already occurred to you that much of the time spent in using this technique is in creating meaningful words from the translated letters. In one case, for area codes, we've made the effort to prepare some standard translations in advance.

But we can actually prepare, in advance, a translation for *every* number: all one-digit numbers, all two-digit numbers, and so on. Of course that seems like a monumental task. It isn't really, but the important question is, how useful would it actually be.

Experience has shown that it pays to create standard word translations for at least all one- and two-digit numbers. These standard translations can be especially useful when it comes to memorizing times and dates.

But if you give it a bit more thought, you'll realize that when you are done translating every number from 1 to 99 you'll end up with a new set of 99 peg words. And you know by now how valuable peg words can be! Since you can—if you like—create an unlimited number of standard translations with the Numerical Code System, you now realize that this powerful technique can give you an *unlimited number of permanent pegs*, which you can use to memorize anything you want, and in proper order!

Okay, now calm down. We're only going to do the first 99 numbers. After you've finished this program you can always do more, if you like.

EXERCISE 5: You can make up your own numerical code peg words for 1 through 99. Or you can borrow from my list. Or you can do a bit of both. But don't just accept mine without checking them. Then study them. Don't worry too much about memorizing them all immediately. The best way to learn them is by using them. But be sure to get a strong concrete image of each.

1. tie	6. jaw	11. tot
2. Noah	7. key	12. tin
3. ma	8. foe	13. tomb
4. rye	9. pa	14. tire
5. law	10. toes	15. towel

16. dish
17. dog
18. dove
19. tub
20. nose
21. net
22. nun
23. name
24. Nero
25. nail
26. notch
27. neck
28. knife
29. knob
30. mouse
31. mat
32. money
33. mummy
34. mower
35. mule
36. match
37. mug
38. movie
39. mop
40. rose
41. rat
42. rain
43. ram

44. rower
45. roll
46. roach
47. rock
48. roof
49. rope
50. lace
51. lad
52. lane
53. lamb
54. lair
55. lily
56. leech
57. log
58. lava
59. lip
60. cheese
61. sheet
62. chain
63. chime
64. cherry
65. jail
66. cha-cha
67. chalk
68. chef
69. ship
70. case
71. cot

72. can
73. comb
74. car
75. coal
76. cage
77. coke
78. cave
79. cob
80. fuse
81. fat
82. fan
83. foam
84. fur
85. file
86. fish
87. fog
88. fife
89. fob
90. bus
91. bat
92. bone
93. bum
94. bear
95. bell
96. beach
97. book
98. puff
99. pipe

Notice that I avoided using "tea" for the number 1, so as not to confuse it with the alphabet word peg for the letter "t." Similarly, I did not use "shoe" for the number 6 since I used it previously for my number rhyme peg for the number 2. I tried, in each case, to use the most concrete, memorable word for each.

Now let's see how to apply this technique to remembering appointments and schedules. Let's decide to represent each day of the week with a single digit, as follows:

1 = Monday	5 = Friday
2 = Tuesday	6 = Saturday
3 = Wednesday	7 = Sunday
4 = Thursday	

Note that I've started with Monday, which is *not* what most calendars do. However, when people think of the "beginning of the week" they are thinking of Monday, aren't they?

Suppose you wanted to represent "Thursday at 3:00." You could use the two-digit number 43, where the digit 4 represents Thursday and the digit 3 represents 3:00. But since your numerical peg word for 43 is **ram,** you can use the image of a **ram**—horns and all—to represent **Thursday at 3:00.** If you create a mental image involving a **ram,** since you will know it is one of your numerical peg words, you will know that it can represent only one thing: Thursday at 3:00.

Here is another example. Consider the numerical peg word **cage.** Its numerical equivalent is 76, which represents Sunday at 6:00. Similarly, the numerical peg word **tub** corresponds to 19 and therefore Monday at 9:00. If I then use **cage** in some fantasy I will always know that it represents Sunday at 6:00, and if I use **tub** it will mean Monday at 9:00.

Now, isn't that easy? There are a few little questions to deal with, of course.

The first is how to handle A.M. and P.M. The simplest answer is to do nothing special; just let the *context* of the situation guide you. For example, if I visualize "my **dentist** standing in a **tub** as he works on me" it will remind me that I've got a dental appointment on Monday at 9:00. As it isn't likely to be 9:00 P.M., I know that it must be 9:00 A.M.

However, you can always attach some special word to the mental image that will represent A.M., for example. You don't need to do it for both A.M. and P.M., since knowing one means you will know the other. You might, for instance, include **white** in your image to represent A.M. times, or **black** to represent P.M. times. So in the previous example my fantasy would be "my **dentist** standing in a **white tub** as he works on me."

Another question is how to handle minutes. One way is just to round everything off to the nearest fifteen-minute interval, quarter, half, or three-quarters past the hour. For those you can use the standard images we talked about earlier when discussing fractions. So you might use **25-cent piece, half grapefruit,** and **three-quarter coat.**

Another way of dealing with minutes is to use the same method I suggested earlier for other types of fractions. That is, imagine the peg word **inside a thimble.** In the context of time, you will of course know that it represents "minutes" and not a "fraction."

So, back to my dentist example. Since **roach** is our numerical peg word for 46, my appointment for Monday at 9:46 A.M. could be represented by "my **dentist** standing in a **white tub** as he works on me, while his assistant stands by holding a **thimble** with a **roach** inside." Can you picture that scene?

The last question to resolve is how to handle 10:00, 11:00, and 12:00. These are a problem because they are the only ones that normally require two digits to represent.

Now, 10:00 is easy because you can simply assign the digit 0, which we haven't yet used, to represent it. So Monday at 10:00 would be "10," or **toes,** and Tuesday at 10:00 would be "20," or **nose.** Here are all of them:

Monday at 10:00—**toes**	Friday at 10:00—**lace**
Tuesday at 10:00—**nose**	Saturday at 10:00—**cheese**
Wednesday at 10:00—**mouse**	Sunday at 10:00—**case**
Thursday at 10:00—**rose**	

Finally, for 11:00 and 12:00 of each day the best solution is to use a three-digit number. That means creating some new special peg words. For example, Sunday at 12:00, which is represented numerically by the three-digit number 712, could be assigned the peg word **kitten.** Then, whenever you use **kitten** for a time period you will know that it must represent Sunday at 12:00. Here is a suggested list of peg words for all of the 11:00 and 12:00 time slots:

Day	11:00	12:00
Monday	**dotted**	**titan**
Tuesday	**knotted**	**antenna**
Wednesday	**matted**	**mitten**
Thursday	**rotate**	**rotten**
Friday	**lighted**	**Aladdin**
Saturday	**cheated**	**jitney**
Sunday	**cadet**	**kitten**

EXERCISE 6: Practice your "time-slot peg words" by saying each one to yourself (or out loud) and visualizing the image. Start with the beginning of your week (e.g., Monday, 6:00 A.M.) and go right through to the end (e.g., Sunday, 11:00 P.M.).

First do it just by the hour. Then do it a second time using half-hour intervals. Then do it a third time using quarter-hour intervals. Do it carefully each time, being sure to visualize the image clearly in your mind.

EXERCISE 7: Write down six appointments you have next week (make some up if you have to). Create a mental image to remember each of the appointments, just as I did in the above example with my dentist.

BREAK POINT

EXERCISE 8: Recall your schedule of six appointments that you memorized in the last exercise. Can you see that with a little practice you can soon throw away your appointment book?

Birthdays and other dates can be handled in a similar way. For each of the months we can assign a one-digit or two-digit number, starting with 1 for January, 2 for February and so on. Similarly, for each day of the month we need either a one-digit or two-digit number.

For the year we need use only a two-digit number, for the context of the situation should tell us whether it's 1875 or 1975.

Since we already have a peg word for each one- and two-digit number, we automatically have a peg word for each month, day, and year!

The only real problem is knowing whether the one- or two-digit number in our fantasy represents the month, the day, or the year. Hopefully you will be able to figure it out from the context. In some cases, however, it can be confusing if you can't distinguish among them.

Suppose, for example, you had an image involving the peg words **pa**, **foe**, and **tot**, such as "my **pa's foe** is that little **tot**." You know that the three peg words translate to 9, 8, and 11, and that it's a date. But it could be any one of several dates, such as August 9, 1911, or September 8, 1911, or November 9, 1918, etc. In fact, in this example there are six different possibilities.

You can set up a special way to identify months, days, and years in a way similar to the way we distinguished between A.M. and P.M.

A good image to use for the **month** is the **moon**, which is in fact how a month was originally defined (a full cycle of the moon takes one month). You can likewise assign the **sun** to represent the **day**, since the sun rises and sets in a single day, and a **ear** to represent the **year** (they rhyme!).

Returning to the example mentioned above, if you wanted to represent the date August 9, 1911, you could associate the peg word **foe** (8 =

August) with the **moon** (month), **pa** (9) with the **sun** (day), and **tot** (11) with an **ear** (year). You might, then, use the following fantasy: "My **pa**, riding on the **sun**, does battle with that little **tot**, who rides an enormous **ear**. They meet on the **moon, foe** to foe!"

(Remember, these fantasies don't go over well in print. But when you think of them yourself they'll work for you).

You can extend the example further. Suppose the date, August 9, 1911, were your mother's birthday. Then you could easily add the phrase "while my mother keeps score by adding candles to a cake." That last phrase would remind you that the date represents her birthday. And if it were your *father's* birthday instead, the phrase could be modified to "while *his father* keeps score . . ." And if it were your parents' anniversary instead? Try "while my mother keeps score by counting wedding rings." You get the idea.

EXERCISE 9: Memorize the following dates and their significance. After a few minutes cover up the list and write them down on a separate piece of paper. Then check to see how well you did.

1. A new client's birthday: September 16.
2. Your secretary's wedding anniversary: February 1.
3. Thomas Jefferson's birthday: April 13.
4. John F. Kennedy's birthday: May 29.
5. Coronation of Queen Elizabeth: June 2, 1953.
6. Thomas Edison unveiled the phonograph: November 29, 1877.
7. John Lennon shot: December 8, 1980.
8. Max Schmeling knocked out Joe Louis: June 19, 1936.

EXERCISE 10: In your notebook write down six dates that you don't already have memorized and their significance in your life. Then commit them to memory. Finally, practice recalling them over the next several days to store them permanently in your long-term memory.

Date	Significance of the Date
1.	
2.	
3.	
4.	
5.	
6.	

DAY 13

REVIEW AND PRACTICE

You've spent the last few days sharpening your memory skills dramatically. You have learned some powerful techniques for memorizing all sorts of information, from driving directions to 14-digit numbers. Specifically, you've learned to

- practice Mental Rehearsal to implant behavior patterns in your mind.
- make use of rhymes and sayings to make bits of information more memorable.
- find and create patterns in geography, words, and numbers.
- apply the powerful Numerical Code System to translate numerical information to verbal information, and then to mental images.

Except for the Numerical Code System, these are all natural activities that you've probably been using to some extent all of your life. But you might not have thought much about them, or tried to use them as deliberate techniques. You can now see how powerful these methods can be when treated as a *skill* that you can practice and improve.

A particular advantage of Mental Rehearsal, for instance, is that you can train your mind even if you can't train your body. You can do this even in cases where you would think that "muscle memory" is the most important component.

Take the case of playing the piano. I know that I've personally experienced "muscle memory," for after practicing a new piece for a while I find that my fingers seem to know what to do. I no longer have to look at the music score. With more practice, in fact, I don't even have to *think* about the score. It's as though my fingers have learned what to do.

Despite this muscle memory, I've found Mental Rehearsal still valuable, to memorize the piece more strongly without a keyboard, by mentally going over the finger action.

Even in the beginning, when learning a new piece for the first time, you can just read the score and mentally rehearse the fingering. I'm sure you've either done it yourself or have seen someone on the bus doing it!

There can be a danger of misusing Mental Rehearsal. Suppose, for example, you memorize a piano piece without using a keyboard. And suppose that you memorize it well, but incorrectly. Because you've not yet played it, you don't have the benefit of the auditory feedback—those sour notes—to warn you of your errors.

So don't get into the habit of using Mental Rehearsal exclusively. In fact, as I've repeated throughout this program, do not depend on any single technique to the exclusion of the others. Your goal should be to enrich your memory skills with *lots* of good techniques.

Rhymes and sayings are well-known memory aids. They exist in every culture, and in every generation. They've been used to remember rules of grammar ("I before e, except after c"), whom to vote for ("I like Ike"), what product to buy ("It's the real thing"), and so on. You can be sure that the reason advertising companies use catchy phrases and rhymes is that they know they work. It's much easier to remember "Don't squeeze the Charmin" than to remember "Buy Charmin toilet tissue."

You can look for rhymes and sayings in situations, or you can look to create them yourself. For example, suppose while you were driving to work you realized that it's St. Valentine's Day and you've got to pick up a card and flowers for your wife on your way home. Also, that she asked you to buy a quart of milk and a half dozen eggs. Now, you're driving the car so you can't write these things down. But in any case, it's more fun—and good practice—to concoct some silly rhyme like:

> A quart and a half
> Plus a rose and a laugh

This should remind you of the **quart** of milk, a **half**-dozen eggs, flowers **(rose)** and a card **(laugh)**.

As for patterns, they exist everywhere: in words, in numbers, in geography, in the way things are organized. You just have to be open to seeing them. And you can always create them yourself. It's just a matter of giving a special meaning to something that doesn't seem to have any.

For example, when I was assigned a locker number and combination lock at a health club I joined, I had to figure out a way to memorize the numbers. Combination number 4-31-18 and locker number 90. Here's what happened, quite spontaneously. The first thing that came to mind was my sister, who's 31 but looks much younger. Starting with that pattern I created this: "For **(4) 31** she looks **18,** and still will when she's **90.**"

Finally, we looked at the powerful Numerical Code System. You could easily be tempted to learn this technique and none other, for it has so many uses. Unfortunately, however, not everyone is completely comfortable with numbers, which the technique relies on. Many, in fact, have a common ailment called "math anxiety."

But even if you are completely comfortable with numbers, there are other reasons for not using the Numerical Code System to the exclusion of the other techniques. One is that it isn't very useful when it comes to remembering names and faces, or speeches, stories, and reading material. Another is that in some cases it would be overkill—a simpler method would be easier. Still another reason is that you want to be able to create mental images *quickly*, and then forget them as soon as they are no longer useful. To do this you've got to have several techniques so that you can use the first one that seems most appropriate instead of trying to force-fit some particular technique.

The most important point, however, is that by being skilled in a variety of techniques you maintain a *rich reservoir* of memory abilities. This also enriches your overall creativity, which in turn makes life more interesting as it increases your ability to learn new things.

You can often use these techniques together. For example, you can use Mental Rehearsal and the Numerical Code System together to memorize each day's schedule. It's best to set this up the day before, then practice it in the evening and again in the morning just before the day begins. Set up your schedule using the Numerical Code System, but then mentally rehearse your day by vividly picturing how you'll carry out each of your activities.

You can also make rhymes and (silly) sayings out of the letters you get after translating with the Numerical Code. Or you can use the letters to create acronyms. For instance, in the example of my health club lock and locker numbers, 4-31-18 and 90, if you translate each digit individually you get the letters R M T T F P S, which you might just memorize as a sentence by giving it a meaning such as "reach more than the first physician said."

EXERCISE 1: By now you should be able to make up your own exercises to practice your new skills. This is something you will be doing, hopefully, the rest of your life!

Make up some numbers at random, numbers of varying lengths from say 6 to 20 digits. Then use different techniques to memorize them: first look for patterns or significance, then use the numerical code, alone or combined with acronyms. Try to increase your speed by memorizing them in less and less time. Then work on increasing your power by lengthening the numbers that you memorize. Spend about 20 minutes right now making up and practicing various such exercises.

BREAK POINT

EXERCISE 2: Make up and do some exercises to practice memorizing some telephone numbers, schedules, and dates. Spend about 20 minutes doing that right now.

BREAK POINT

Now for some long-term projects.

EXERCISE 3: Over the next several weeks you're going to gradually memorize your calendar or appointment book, for as far into the future as you normally keep it. Get it out now and *plan* how you'll go about doing this. Set a long-term goal of, say, four weeks from today when you'll give up the book entirely and rely on your memory only!

EXERCISE 4: Over the next several weeks you're going to gradually memorize your entire Rolodex (or name/address/phone book). Get it out now and design your plan. You need to first set a goal, on the basis of how extensive it is, for when you'll have it all memorized. Then break down your goal into smaller stages, such as by a particular date you will have all the A's memorized, then by another date the B's, and so on. Lay out this schedule in detail. Write it down in your calendar book (later you'll have the plan memorized too!).

Congratulations! You've come a long way since beginning this program. But you're near the end now. Just one more day to wrap everything up, put it all in perspective, and make a final assessment of your progress.

DAY 14

COMPLETE PROGRAM SUMMARY

We started on Day 1 by agreeing to treat memory as a skill. By now you've no doubt increased that skill considerably. You understand the importance of the Basic Memory Principles of association, imagination, and organization, and how they make the memory techniques effective. You also know how to apply the various techniques to solve all sorts of common memory problems.

I'm sure that you also understand how a powerful memory can increase your success, whether in business, relationships with others, or your own personal happiness. No more missed appointments. No more forgetting where you put things. No more scraps of written reminders. No more forgetting who's who and what's what. You can replace embarrassment, excuses, and forgetfulness with confidence, dependability, and respect.

By way of summarizing these powerful techniques, below is a table listing all of the techniques and the situations in which they can be applied. They are listed in the same order as we tackled them.

Applications marked with an asterisk (*) are other areas in which the technique can be applied—they were not originally discussed for that technique during the program but you can now figure them out for yourself. Take some time to explore them on your own.

Memory Technique	Memory Application Area
Link System	List of things in order
	"To do" list in order
	* Linking used in almost every area
Number Rhyme System	List of things in any order
	"To do" list in any order

Alphabet System	List of things in any order
	"To do" list in any order
	Spelling of troublesome words
	* New words
	* New names
	* Bits of fact and trivia
Roman Room System	Speeches
	Jokes and stories
	* List of things in any order
	* "To do" list in any order
	* Reading
	* Listening
	* Preparing for an exam
	* Preparing a presentation
Mind mapping	Reading
	Listening
	Preparing for an exam
	Preparing a presentation
	* Speeches
	* Jokes and stories
	* Organizing ideas before writing
Word substitution	New words
	New names
Dominant feature	Faces
	Matching faces, names, and jobs
Mental rehearsal	Packing for a trip
	Getting chores done
	Performing in public
	Locating lost items
	* Finding your way
Rhymes and sayings	Bits of fact and trivia
	* New words
	* New names
	* Spelling of troublesome words
Physical patterns	Finding your way
	* Locating lost items
	* Bits of fact and trivia
Word patterns	Bits of fact and trivia
	* New words
	* New names
	* Memorizing poetry

Number patterns	Numbers, prices, and phone numbers
	Appointments, schedules, and dates
Numerical code system	Numbers, prices, and phone numbers
	Appointments, schedules, and dates
	* List of things in any order
	* "To do" list in any order
	* Speeches
	* Jokes and stories
	* Preparing for an exam
	* Preparing a presentation

Finally, below is a list of the techniques organized by area of application. You may find this list handy to help you decide on the best technique to use for a particular memory problem.

It's a good idea to keep this list up to date. Add to it as you develop your own techniques and variations, and different ways to apply them.

Memory Problem	Technique (page number)
Appointments	Number Patterns (129)
	Numerical Code System (137)
Bits of fact and trivia	Alphabet System (53)
	Physical Patterns (125)
	Rhymes and Sayings (123)
	Word Patterns (127)
Chores	Any of the "List Techniques" (see under "Lists")
	Mental Rehearsal (115)
Dates	Number Patterns (129)
	Numerical Code System (137)
Faces (matching names, etc.)	Alphabet System (53)
	Dominant Feature (92)
	Rhymes and Sayings (123)
	Word Patterns (127)
	Word Substitution (89)
Finding lost items	Mental Rehearsal (115)
	Physical Patterns (125)
Finding your way	Mental Rehearsal (115)
	Physical Patterns (125)

Memory Problem	Technique (page number)
Listening	Mental Rehearsal (115)
	Mind Mapping (81)
	Numerical Code System (137)
	Roman Room System (71)
Lists, in order only	Link System (33)
Lists, in any order	Alphabet System (53)
	Number Rhyme System (43)
	Numerical Code System (137)
	Roman Room System (71)
New Words and Names	Alphabet System (53)
	Rhymes and Sayings (123)
	Word Patterns (127)
	Word Substitution (89)
Numbers	Number Patterns (129)
	Numerical Code System (137)
Phone Numbers	Number Patterns (129)
	Numerical Code System (137)
Prices	Number Patterns (129)
	Numerical Code System (137)
Schedules	Number Patterns (129)
	Numerical Code System (137)
Speaking	Mental Rehearsal (115)
	Mind Mapping (81)
	Numerical Code System (137)
	Roman Room System (71)
Reading	Mental Rehearsal (115)
	Mind Mapping (81)
	Numerical Code System (137)
	Roman Room System (71)
Rules of Spelling, Grammar	Alphabet System (53)
	Rhymes and Sayings (123)
Writing	Mind Mapping (81)
	Roman Room System (71)

NOTE: Linking is used almost everywhere. So are the Basic Memory Principles of association, imagination, and organization.

HOW GOOD IS YOUR MEMORY NOW?

Instructions

As you did in the beginning of this program, you will take a test to determine your present memory capabilities. Be sure that you are sitting in a comfortable place and will not be interrupted for about an hour. Turn back to that first test on page 14, and try the test again.

Most people take their memory for granted and assume they can't do anything to improve it. You, on the other hand, have worked hard to develop new skills. As a result you've boosted your memory power by deliberate practice of proven techniques!

If you didn't do well because you perhaps didn't have the time to work on the techniques, then you can always go back and start over. Make up your own exercises if you're tired of mine. But learn the techniques and *use them*.

This is not the end, but the beginning. From here on you have begun a new way of using your mind. As you apply the memory techniques your memory power will continue to increase, and you'll continue to become a more creative thinker as well. This, in turn, will make your memory even more effective. But most important, "remembering" has now become something to enjoy, as an interesting game, rather than as a chore.

I'd be pleased to hear from those who have developed their own variations on the techniques, or other interesting applications. You can write to me directly at:

Eric M. Bienstock & Associates
231 East 76th Street, 1G
New York, NY 10021

RECOMMENDED READING LIST

Memory Skills

Benne, Bart. *Waspleg and Other Mnemonics*. Dallas: Taylor Publishing Co., 1988.

Buzan, Tony. *Use Your Perfect Memory*. New York: E. P. Dutton, 1984.

Furst, Bruno. *Stop Forgetting*. New York: Greenberg, 1949.

Furst, Bruno. *The Practical Way to a Better Memory*. Greenwich, CT: Fawcett, 1944.

Hamilton, Stephen F. *Mastering Your Memory*. New York: Gramercy Publishing, 1947.

Kellett, Michael C. *How to Improve Your Memory and Concentration*. New York: Monarch Press, 1977.

Lapp, Danielle C. *Don't Forget!* New York: McGraw-Hill, 1987.

Lorayne, Harry. *Memory Makes Money*. Boston: Little, Brown, 1988.

Lorayne, Harry, and Jerry Lucas. *The Memory Book*. New York: Ballantine Books, 1974.

Minninger, Joan. *Total Recall*. New York: Pocket Books, 1986.

Roth, David M. *Roth Memory Course*. New York: The Sun Dial Press, 1918.

Slung, Michele. *The Absent-Minded Professor's Memory Book*. New York: Ballantine Books, 1985.

Werner, Victor. *Short-Cut Memory*. New York: Cowles, 1968.

Related Creativity and Thinking Skills

Bienstock, Eric M. *Thinking: A Special Report*. New York: Boardroom Reports, 1988.

de Bono, Edward. *Lateral Thinking: Creativity Step by Step*. New York: Harper & Row, 1970.

Guilford, J. P. *Way Beyond the IQ*. Buffalo, NY: The Creative Education Foundation, 1977.

Osborn, Alex. *Applied Imagination*. New York: Scribner's, 1963.

Peters, Roger. *Practical Intelligence*. New York: Harper & Row, 1987.

Silva, Jose and Philip Miele. *The Silva Mind Control Method*. New York: Pocket Books, 1977.

von Oech, Roger. *A Whack on the Side of the Head*. New York: Warner Books, 1983.

Wonder, Jacquelyn, and Priscilla Donovan. *Whole-Brain Thinking*, New York: Ballantine Books, 1984.